Introduction to
Computer Forensics

Introduction to
Computer Forensics
With 33 Real Life Cases

Gordon Pelton

BIKERACE PRESS, California, USA

Visit www.CreateSpace.com to order additional copies.

ISBN: 978-1-46097085-0

DEDICATION

To Gayle, my wife and best friend, I owe more than could ever be expressed. You have always supported my projects with patience, understanding and encouragement. You have done the same through the many hours I spent working on this book. With great love and caring, I dedicate this book to you.

Contents

ACKNOWLEDGMENT

I would like to thank an unknown attorney who I met on a ski lift at the Northstar Ski Resort near Lake Tahoe in Northern California during the winter of 1991. We found ourselves seated next to each other for the five minute ride to the top of the Comstock Run. During our brief conversation on that short ride, this attorney introduced me to "Computer Forensics." Up until that time I had never heard the term. Within the next year I had obtained the training that, when added to my already forty-six year career, three in electronics and forty-three as a Computer Scientist, enabled me to begin a new career as a Computer Forensics Expert Witness. I never learned that attorney's name but I owe him a debt of gratitude. Thank you, friend.

COMPUTER FORENSICS

Computer forensics is the science and art of discovery, preservation, extraction, analysis, interpretation, presentation and explanation of evidence that exists on digital devices.

Preface

I was first introduced to computers in 1957 as a college senior majoring in mathematics. From that day until this, I have participated in the computer revolution, the whole time fascinated as I watched computers work their way further and further into our everyday activities. That encroachment is ongoing and it may never end.

As I write this, computers are already so ingrained into the human personal and workaday world that it is not surprising that, just as we search file cabinets for records and documentation of past events, we are now compelled to also search computers and other digital media. In a simple way, the field of computer forensics has been developed to guide and aid in these computer searches.

This book is intended to introduce the reader to the art and science of computer forensics. To help explain how computer forensics is applied in real life situations, thirty-three computer forensics cases are described. These are actual cases, cases in which computer forensics has played an important role.

Though much of what is discussed in these pages is applicable to any type of digital device, this book concentrates primarily on the application of computer forensics to computers – that's where computer forensics is most often required and most often applied. And because much of computer forensics is practiced on computers running a Windows operating system, most of what is discussed here is directly applicable to Windows Operating

Systems (but much is also applicable in a general way to other operating systems).

It is not necessary to read this book from cover to cover to benefit from the information presented within. The book has been designed to be used as a short reference document. The book's Table of Contents will guide you to various sections and topics that are intended to be more or less self-contained. You may want refer to the book from time to time when you have questions regarding computer forensics.

Chapter 1 introduces the subject of computer forensics and covers its uses and areas of application. Chapters 2, 4, 6, 9 and 11 present thirty three real life computer forensic cases. Chapter 3 concentrates on digital evidence and its sources. It includes a discussion of email as evidence. Chapters 5, 7 and 8 describe some of the many ways in which users with something to hide attempt to protect, conceal or destroy digital evidence. Chapter 10 talks about the conduct and results of a computer forensics examination. Chapter 12 discusses the need to use a trained and certified expert for computer forensics examinations and what might happen if untrained or uncertified professional are used instead. Finally, the Appendix (Glossary) provides definitions of a few frequently encountered technical terms used in computer forensics. At the end of the book you will find an extensive index to help you find the pages where particular subjects are mentioned.

Chapter

1

Computer Forensics

General

Computers are more intricately involved in our everyday lives today in ways that we could not even have imagined forty, or thirty, or even twenty-five years ago. Although the first  digital computers were built in the forties and used by the military, it was not until the middle to late fifties that they began to appear commercially. (During the Second World War the U. S. military used computers for calculating the trajectories of projectiles from large guns). In the fifties, a single computer cost millions of dollars. The development of the microchip (integrated circuit) in the sixties and seventies created a revolution in the computer industry, one result of which has been the availability of inexpensive, small computers.

Since the appearance of the personal computer in the mid nineteen seventies, the use of computers has grown to unanticipated proportions. A large percentage of American households have at least one computer and many have more. Most American companies, whether large or small, could not conduct daily operations without the help of computers – in many cases hundreds or thousands of them. Our educational institutions, all the way from the tiniest elementary school up to our most advanced universities, make thousands upon thousands of computers available to students. Our governmental agencies employ people by the hundreds of thousands and a large percentage of those employees use computers in their everyday work.

A recent statistic informs us that in the United States alone there are from half a billion to a billion or more computers in government, corporations, households and schools. Computers have become a way of life in America and

> **COMPUTERS IN THE USA**
>
> **OVER HALF A BILLION IN:**
> - **GOVERNMENT**
> - **CORPORATIONS**
> - **HOUSEHOLDS**
> - **SCHOOLS**
>
> **USED BY 150 MILLION ADULTS**

every day more and more of us are learning to use them. More that 125 million adults use computers daily in our personal lives or in our work or school. If honest, everyday citizens going about their daily lives employ computers to facilitate their tasks, it stands to reason that criminals do the same.

It is not surprising that we are becoming a society that relies heavily on electronic communication and electronic documents. Ninety-three percent of all corporate communication in this country is done via email and other electronic means. That includes not only memos and emails but also personal notes and working papers, reports and studies -- documents of all types. Only thirty-five percent of that ever gets printed. Sixty-five percent of all corporate communication never exists in any form other than electronic – that is, it exists only in digital form.

CORPORATE DOCUMENTS

- **93% is electronic (ie: computer)**
- **Only 35% ever gets printed**
- **65% exists only on computers**

And while the statistics are lower for individuals, the trend for private email and other communication, as well as planning, banking, individual research and shopping, is moving in the same direction.

It isn't only in the United States that all this is happening: computer usage is growing in many other countries at the same rate as in the U.S. Almost everyone in civilized countries -- and we now know, in some uncivilized countries -- use computers in every aspect of life.

The NASA photo of Figure 1-1 shows our world at night. What you can so clearly see from this composite satellite picture are the many lighted population areas of the world where electricity is most heavily used. It is safe to assume that where there is electricity and where there are lights, there are also computers and people who use them.

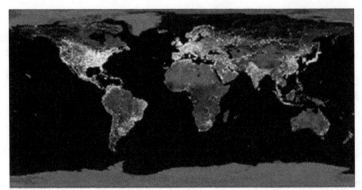

Figure 1-1   NASA Satellite Photo of the World

For those of us here in the United States and for others around the globe, the digital computer has been firmly assimilated into nearly every aspect of our lives. This explosive trend is expected to continue, probably without end. Is it surprising, then, that the content of computer memory is increasingly becoming important in both criminal and civil investigations?

Application of Computer Forensics

Information contained in a computer could be required for use in a court of law, a civil proceeding or an administrative action. It could be used by criminal prosecutors, civil litigators (on either side of the aisle), law enforcement officials, corporate management or by companies or individuals.

In the criminal area, the need for evidence from computers by both the prosecution and the defense spans every type of crime imaginable – all the way from petty theft to murder. Criminals, just like the rest of us, use computers in many ways. They use it to communicate among themselves, to store and process financial information, or to plan or record their crimes. When a crime is committed, the probability exists that evidence of the crime could be found on some computer somewhere.

COMPUTER FORENSICS USED BY

- **Prosecutors**
- **Criminal Defense Attorneys**
- **Civil Litigators**
- **Insurance Companies**
- **Corporations**
- **Law Enforcement**

Computer forensics is also used in civil litigation. With most of corporate America conducting so much of their business only by computer, both sides of almost any civil case would likely require computer-borne evidence to support their case. In the recent Microsoft Antitrust case, for example, several emails that passed among Microsoft executives (including Bill Gates) were used to show Microsoft's alleged intention to violate antitrust legislation.

We are all aware of the recent troubles at Enron, Arthur Anderson, Worldcom and others. These are examples in the business world where official investigative bodies have searched corporate computers for evidence of wrongdoing. Other situations might involve misuse of computers by employees – employees who could be involved in such activities as embezzlement, theft of company secrets, sexual harassment, possession of pornography, misappropriation of company assets or even of company time.

Many companies have written policies against use of the company's computers for personal or illegal activities. Notwithstanding written policies, and considering the fact that computers are so available in the corporate world, one would expect that some corporate employees would never-the-less be using company computers for their own private purposes. Consider the notion of employees downloading pornographic images to their work computers. It's astounding how much of that goes on right under the noses of corporate management.

Besides the potential legal and civil liabilities that a company risks, such activities by employees can cost thousands of dollars just due to the misappropriation of company time. Thousands of companies call upon computer forensics experts every year to search their company's computers in an effort to stop such practices.

With so many private citizens using computers, individual citizens often have need of computer forensics to help bring facts to the fore in cases

CRIMES IN THE USA

- **300 million population**
- **15 million victims/year**
- **145 milliion crimes/year**
- **Many involve computers?**

of personal litigation. Common examples would include divorce cases where the relevant activities or financial manipulations of one or both parties are documented in their company or home computer. These areas are discussed in later chapters.

Computer Forensics and Crime

The U.S. Bureau of Justice Statistics tells us that there are almost three-hundred million people in the United States and that five percent of those become victims of crime each year. That equates to about one-hundred and forty-five million crimes every year in the U.S. alone.

How many of those crimes involve a computer? Since computers have become ubiquitous, are sold as commodities, and serve us like huge filing cabinets, you can guess that the answer is very large.

CRIMINAL EVIDENCE

- DRUG DEALERS' TRANSACTION LEDGERS
- PORNOGRAPHY ADS ONLINE
- FRAUD SCHEMES ADVERTISED ONLINE
- GRAPHICS FOR COUNTERFEIT BILLS
- FORGED CASHIERS CHECKS
- FORGED CERTIFICATES
- CO-CONSPIRATORS' EMAIL
- PLANS AND TO-DO LISTS FOR CRIMES
- WEB BROWSING HISTORY

Here are just a few crimes in which computer forensics plays a major role: murder, fraud, narcotics traffic, credit card theft, identity theft, computer network hacking, pedophilia, pornography, copyright piracy, industrial espionage, sexual harassment, and more. Computers are used to download, store and display child pornography or to prepare and transmit threatening email messages. In cases involving fraud, a computer is often used to maintain financial records, schedules, contact lists, diaries and action plans.

But no matter what the crime, there are three ways that computers can be involved. First, a computer can be the target of a crime, as when a hacker breaks into a commercial or government computer network and steals information -- credit card numbers for example.

CRIMES INVOLVING COMPUTERS

- Murder
- Fraud
- Narcotics Traffic
- Credit Card Theft
- Computer Hacking
- Paedophilia
- Pornography
- Copyright Piracy
- Industrial Espionage
- Sexual Harassment

Second, the computer can be used in the commission of a crime – as when it is used in embezzlement or to commit wire fraud. If a person downloads kiddy-porn from the Internet, sends a blackmailing email to another person or posts a fraudulent item for sale on Ebay, he or she is using a computer in the commission of a crime.

CRIMINALS USE COMPUTERS TO

- PLAN THEIR CRIMES
- COMMUNICATE AMONG THEMSELVES
- STORE FINANCIAL INFORMATION
- DEFRAUD OTHERS ON INTERNET
- BREAK INTO OTHER COMPUTERS
- MANY OTHERS

Third, a computer may contain evidence of a crime. Computers so often document our very thoughts, our dreams, our plans and activities, our research or our communications. Criminal examples might include a pedophile downloading pornographic images to his computer or someone using his computer to search the Internet for ways to make a murder appear accidental.

For some crimes all three apply. Consider the case of a hacker breaking into a commercial network. His computer is used to commit the crime, a network computer is the target of the crime, and both his computer and the target computer (and perhaps other intermediate computers as well) contain evidence of the crime.

Corporate Computer Forensics

I have already mentioned the use of computer forensics at Enron, Worldcom and others who have recently been in the news. The scandals perpetrated by management at these companies represent some of the most extreme abuses of trust discovered in recent history.

EMPLOYEES' COMPUTER MISUSE

- EMAIL FRIENDS
- SWAP JOKES
- HARASS OTHERS
- PLAN VACATIONS
- SURF THE WEB
- DOWNLOAD PORN
- SABOTAGE INFO
- SABOTAGE SYSTEMS
- EMBEZZLE FUNDS, INTELLECTUAL PROPERTY, OR PROPRIETARY INFO

We all hope that such occurrences are rare. Perhaps just as important are the many abuses occurring daily at companies around the world by employees at all levels.

Fifty percent of workers in the western world use computers on a daily basis. That creates a lot of opportunity for employee misuse of computers. Technology is changing so rapidly that it is impossible for companies to anticipate every threat

Fifty percent of workers in the western world use computers on a daily basis. That creates a lot of opportunity for employee misuse of computers. Technology is changing so rapidly that it is impossible for companies to anticipate every threat.

Companies use Computer Forensics to:

- Support civil litigation
- Track hackers
- Prove employee misconduct
- Other

The ways in which employees betray the trust put in them by their employers and misuse their employer's computers range all the way from emailing friends to more serious illegal activities. This includes things such as downloading child pornography or stealing the company's intellectual property. In a later chapter you'll find the case of a disgruntled employee who sabotaged his company's network and nearly bankrupted the company.

Some employees have also been known to use their employers' computers to plan vacations, email friends, swap jokes, sexually harass others, sabotage data bases, or embezzle company funds or proprietary information. Any of these activities, no matter how innocent it may seem, includes the misuse of company computers and, perhaps more importantly, of company time.

If employees are conducting questionable activities, how do you prove it? If you have to fire the employee, you must have the facts to back up your actions or you run the risk of a lawsuit. To avoid that, you may need to examine some of the company's computers – the ones used by the employee. The company's IT Department could perhaps do that but if they are not trained in computer forensics you'd run a high risk that any evidence

> **RUBY's SEXY – SHE DOESN'T WORK HERE. BUT:**
>
> **She's really HOT in Marketing, Tech Support and a few other departments**
>
> **There are already 1247 visits to her site today to see her new video**
>
> **Too bad the End-of-Quarter Reports were due and that the network went down from traffic overload**
>
> **I'm sure the CIO will understand....**

obtained would not be admitted in court or other official proceeding.

If an employee is downloading pornography, the employer can be open to blackmail or trouble from law enforcement. In some cases, executives or even board members could be held personally liable for problems created by their employees.

If you have no way to be certain that the Internet is used only for business, and that questionable content, computer viruses, pirated software and bootlegged music are kept off your network, a computer forensic expert can help.

Computer Forensics for Individuals

There are civil cases where an individual's computer may contain information important to a private civil case. For example, John is divorcing Mary and for purposes of the property settlement John claims, falsely, that there are no assets to divide. His computer might provide Mary with evidence that John has transferred assets to hidden accounts or to other

Individuals' Use of Computer Forensics

- **Divorce Property Settlement**
- **Contract Disputes**
- **Other Civil litigation**

people. John may have prepared their income taxes on his computer and copies of his tax forms may still exist there. Or, Jim suspects Joe, his business partner, of diverting company funds. Here too, the evidence in Joe's computer could prove Jim's case.

In any of these situations, whether they are criminal, corporate, or individual, a computer forensics expert can make the difference between success and failure of your cause. Even if the perpetrators make serious attempts to destroy the evidence it's likely that remnants of the activity remain to be found by the trained and diligent computer forensics investigator.

Chapter

2

Computer Forensics Cases

Million Dollar Round Off Error

The case of the million dollar round-off error occurred in the middle sixties when most people were still unfamiliar with computers. And, it wasn't so much a case of an "error" as it was intentional theft. This is the earliest case of computer crime of which I had personal knowledge.

A particular computer programmer, who had worked for a number of years for a large San Francisco bank finally realized he had a huge opportunity. One day just after another programmer had resigned he was assigned to take over maintenance of the computer program that entered banking transactions to the customer accounts database on the bank's mainframe computer. When a bank customer would make a deposit, this was the computer program that entered the deposited amount to that person's account.

Things were going along pretty good for this programmer until after a year or so he got the flu and had to stay home a few days. While he was home nursing his stomach ache some problem with his program turned up. The problem had

to be fixed right away so management assigned another programmer to find out what was wrong. He wouldn't have known it at the time because the title "Computer Forensics Investigator" hadn't even been invented -- but this substitute programmer may have been the first ever to be working under that job description.
.

It didn't take long for the substitute programmer to discover that the errant program was doing something very strange. Normally, at month end, every customer's account would be credited with accrued interest for the month. But this program did something different. Instead of rounding up or rounding down to account for the fraction of a cent of round-off error resulting from nearly every numerical division, this program had been modified by the flu-stricken maintenance programmer to always credit that little extra fraction of a cent to his own personal account.

He was averaging half a cent from each and every one of the thousands of deposit transactions that occurred daily at the bank. Many many dollars were being automatically deposited to his own account in such small increments (less than half a cent with each transaction) that nobody was the wiser. And the bank's books always balanced because those fractions of a penny came from the customers – who, because of the miniscule amounts, never noticed the difference. A very cute little trick.

When he returned from sick leave the guilty programmer went immediately to jail. He did not pass GO. He did not collect two hundred dollars.

Death in a Bathtub

On a peaceful spring morning in 1999 in a small town in South Dakota, the Presbyterian minister leaves the parsonage to say his morning prayers at the church. He tells his wife he'll be back in twenty minutes. Let's call the minister Steve. We'll call his wife Sandy. Steve later tells the police what happened that morning.

On his return, he calls out to Sandy. No answer. He calls again. No answer. Steve, concerned, hurries up the stairs to find Sandy face down in an overflowing bathtub. He's frantic. His heart is pounding. Sandy's unconscious but he can tell she is breathing. Steve can't think. His mind races, his heart pounds but he tries to steady himself; he knows he must do the right thing.

He attempts to grab her under her shoulders to yank her from the tub. He fails. He tries again to heave her from the tub. She's too heavy. He reaches deep into the water underneath her head and yanks the plug. At some point, he doesn't remember when, he turns off the water. He's able to turn her over. He holds hear head out of the water until the tub drains down. Panicked, he calls 911. He's unable to explain later how he could have been so businesslike on the phone.

Within minutes the police and a medical team arrive. Unable to revive her, they take her to the

THE RECORDER & TIMES

Pastor's wife drowns in bathtub

Pastor suspected

hospital. A brain scan shows a flat line -- no brain activity. The medical staff draws a sample of her blood. In distress, Steve phones his two daughters.

The next day, with Steve and the two girls by her bedside, Sandy dies. In his report, the coroner cites the cause of death: drowning.

Police are suspicious. Despite his claimed attempts to wrest Sandy from the overflowing tub, the Reverend's clothes had been dry when the police arrived a few minutes later. The police immediately begin an investigation of the Reverend. They interrogate him and his daughters. They talk with his friends, with members of his church. They review his and the church's phone records.

Police soon learn the Reverend had been seeing a girlfriend in another town. And lately the girlfriend had been putting pressure on him to end his marriage. Frustrated by his delays to seek a divorce, she broke up with him. The police realize they have only circumstantial evidence. Steve, of course, denies he had anything to do with Sandy's drowning. He seems honestly distressed by Sandy's death.

The blood test at the hospital finds enough of the sedative, Temazepam, in Sandy's blood to have knocked her out. Police then learn that Steve had gone to his doctor two weeks before Sandy's death saying he needed something to help him sleep. Steve had even suggested

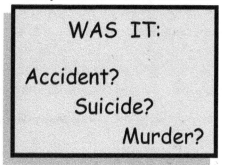

WAS IT:

Accident?
Suicide?
Murder?

Temazepam to the doctor and when he had the doctor's prescription he filled it at one drugstore then went to a second drugstore and told them he had lost the prescription. After checking with the doctor, who confirmed that he had written a prescription for the drug, the second pharmacist provided Steve with even more Temazepam. Several weeks later, two days before Sandy's death, Steve had each of the two prescriptions filled again.

Hoping to find copies of email between Steve and the woman he had been dating, police seize Steve's computer from his church office and pass it on to their computer forensics expert.

In his search of Steve's church computer, the computer forensics expert finds no incriminating email to or from Steve's girlfriend. He does find that just a few weeks before his wife's death Steve had been searching the Internet for surefire but painless ways to kill someone. Steve had obtained information on the Internet about Temazepam (recall the prescription for sleeping pills that Steve had filled four times?).

Still proclaiming his innocence and apparently outraged by accusations against him, Steve is arrested. He's put in jail to await trial while the police and the computer forensics expert continue their investigations.

At trial, the Reverend surprises everyone when he produces a suicide note he claims had been written by

May 13, 1999.

Dear Pam,

I am sorry I ruined your wedding. Your dad told me about your concerns of my interfering in Jill's and the possibility I might ruin hers. I won't be there so put your mind at ease. You will understand after the wedding is done.

I love you all,

Mom

The Suicide Note

Sandy to one of the couple's two adult daughters. We'll call the daughters Pam and Jill. His back straight, his demeanor certain, Steve claims he found the note in a liturgy book in his church office three months after Sandy's death. The note reads as shown.

The computer forensics expert goes back to the Reverend's computer expecting to find evidence that the Reverend had himself written the suicide note. But he finds nothing. Then police learn that after his wife's death, Steve had given his home computer to one of their daughters.

It took police a few days to get that computer but when they had it they immediately had it searched. On that computer the computer forensics expert finds numerous files containing sermons -- and, interleaved among Steve's sermons, a file named *Sandy.doc*.

This file, *Sandy.doc,* contains little text but the text that it does contain shows the identical date and last two lines of the alleged suicide note. The computer forensics expert also finds that there are other similarities between the file named *Sandy.doc* and the suicide note. Both are typed in the same typeface. Both have the same margins set. Both contain the same date with the same missing space before the year; both were signed off with the same closing. And there is more.

May 13,1999.

I love you all,

Mom

Note in File *Sharon.doc*

Metadata[1] (reliable information that is not visible to the casual observer) stored with the file shows not only that the contents of the file was authored by the Reverend but also that it's written three months after the drowning. Differing versions of the note were interleaved with Steve's sermons. Apparently the Reverend sits down at the computer one day, works on the note a while, works on his sermons a while, then on the note again, then on the sermons and so on.

In the end, the jury convicts Reverend Steve of Sandy's murder. The Reverend, so loudly and confidently proclaiming his innocence, didn't even know of the existence of the damning evidence on his computer. Now he's in prison for life.

---

[1] *For a description of Metadata, see the next chapter.*

Sold Out by Friends

Jack and two friends were planning the formation of a new company together. Jack used his employer's laptop not only for work but also in planning the new business. He and his friends exchanged emails almost daily for several months. When their plans were nearly ready, Jack wrote a letter summarizing their agreements. Unfortunately, jack didn't make copies of his communication with the others. Nor did he print a copy of the letter summarizing their deal.

When all was ready, Jack erased the letter and the emails from his employer's laptop computer – then quit his job. All of his communications among his friends were gone – along with the all-important letter.

Excited and looking forward to his new enterprise, Jack and the two friends joined together in their new adventure. It was not to be so exciting for Jack after all though, because after a few months his friends forced Jack out of the new company. Jack decided to sue.

To further his lawsuit against the two friends, Jack needed the emails and that letter. He reasoned that some of it might still exist on the laptop he had used during the planning for the new company but that computer was no longer in Jack's possession. The laptop belonged to his former employer; after contacting his former boss Jack found that someone else had been using it over the intervening few months.

Angered by what was happening to him -- and determined not to be deterred -- Jack somehow convinced the former employer to give him the hard drive from that computer. After several months of use by someone else it was possible, even likely, that much of the evidence he needed for his lawsuit did not survive on the computer.

Never-the-less, Jack engaged a computer forensics expert and this person did succeed in recovering many of the emails. However, the space on the computer that the letter had occupied had been reallocated to another document. Fortunately for Jack the new document was shorter than the letter so the few last paragraphs of the letter survived. These paragraphs were found to contain much of what Jack needed for his lawsuit.

What could have been a total failure turned out to be a success for Jack.

Demoted CEO Steals Database

The founder and CEO of a biomedical research company was demoted by the Board of Directors. We'll call him Bob. Angry, Bob quit his job -- but not before copying and taking with him a proprietary company database and other sensitive files. In violation of his non-disclosure agreement he then approached one of the company's competitors attempting to establish business with them – business that included the pilfered database. Instead of exploiting an unfair advantage, the competitor reported the situation to the Chairman of the original company – who filed a civil suit against their former CEO.

The Board of Directors of his previous employer hired a computer forensics expert to search for evidence of the thefts of proprietary computer data. The computer forensics expert searched Bob's computer at the original company but did not find copies of the files he had stolen. They did, however, find a forgotten TO-DO list that showed Bob had intended to copy the company's one hundred million dollar database for his personal use. They also found a second TO-DO list showing that he had wanted to "learn how to destroy evidence on a computer."

Apparently he wasn't an apt student either because with the fact of the two TO DO lists still present on his computer, Bob was forced to settle the lawsuit on the Board's terms.

Secretary in Business

A sales executive traveled extensively for his company. While he was out of town, his private secretary was running an Internet business from her desk on company time. She was using the company's computer and telephones -- not to mention her own time. The company

MISAPPROPRIATION OF COMPANY ASSETS

- Boss often out of town
- Secretary runs web business from office
- Using company assets
  Telephone
  Computer
  Web connection
  Time
- CF expert searches her computer
- Secretary is fired

became suspicious and called in a computer forensics expert to examine her company computer. It was very easy for him to find a lot of evidence of her Internet dealings and to prove what she was doing.

Needless to say, soon after the computer forensics examination she was no longer employed there. The scary thing is, she may be doing that same thing at another firm at this very moment. I hope it's not mine – or one of yours.

Employee Downloads Pornography

Pornographic files and odd documents such as "The Anarchist's Cookbook" were mysteriously turning up on the company computer network. Management recognized the risk of having this sort of material on its computers. Members of the Board of Directors were unwilling to put either the company's or their personal assets at risk. They called in a computer forensics expert.

He found the culprit was a disgruntled employee who had been turned down for a promotion into the company's Information

Hard Drive

Technology Group. Feeling "dissed," the employee was trying to show them, by downloading these provocative materials, that he knew more about their network than they did. Apparently he did know a lot too; but it didn't save him from termination.

The Missing Employee

Here's a case that occurred more than thirty years ago, long before anyone thought much about computer forensics. Without really knowing that what I was doing was called computer forensics, I was able to use it to nail a culprit. I was Manager of Software Engineering in the IT Division of a well-known company in Silicon Valley in the San Francisco Bay Area. I had an employee, a software engineer, who insisted he would be so much more productive if I would allow him to work the graveyard instead of the day shift. His argument was that so many other programmers were using the computers during the day that his sole use of them during the nighttime hours would make him so much more productive and that would be to everyone's benefit. He even claimed he could work about twelve very productive hours a day that way. I agreed to his plan.

MISSING SOFTWARE ENGINEER

- **Software engineer working nightshift**
- **Wrote glowing progress reports to me**
- **I get complaint from cardroom in town**
- **I search his computer**
- **File date/times show his reports are fraudulent**
- **He's actually working 1-2 hours per night**
- **He's history**

My man was leaving me glowing progress reports each week telling me how much software development he was accomplishing. Then one day I got a strange phone call from the owner of a card-room in town. A card-room is a place you can go twenty-four hours a day to gamble at cards -- they were legal in California then. The owner who phoned me said that this guy, my night-shift employee, owed him hundreds of dollars in gambling losses.

The call aroused my suspicions: how could this guy who was working twelve hours a night at the computer have so much time to spend playing cards in town? I began to search his computer for signs that he really was working during the hours he claimed.

Computers cooperate in searches like this by date/time stamping nearly every action taken during the development and testing of computer programs. Date/time stamps on the computer's hard drive revealed that he would arrive at work about six PM after most everyone else had left for the day. He'd log onto the computer and work for about thirty minutes. The logs showed that he worked again for about twenty minutes starting about five AM.

He had been doing this night after night for two months. The computer evidence was definite. His progress reports were bogus. He was toast.

Husband's Always Online. Why?

A wife sought the help of a computer forensics expert. Seems her husband spent inordinate amounts of time surfing the Internet. She was suspicious. She wanted to know what was going on. What was he doing on the computer for so many hours each day? Had he posted her picture on a questionable site? Was he into chat rooms? Was he having an affair or corresponding with other women? Everyone has heard those stories. Had he gambled away their savings? Had he been recklessly investing their money? She just knew he was hiding something. She wanted to know what.

She called a computer forensics expert. She insisted the investigation be thorough and include all the husband's computers: three desktop computers, two laptops, and hundreds of diskettes and CDs.

The result? He was doing plenty that many people would consider seedy. But nothing more than what she already knew about. That, at least, put her mind at ease.

GORDON PELTON

Chapter

3

Digital/Computer Evidence

Digital Devices

Digital evidence is informati
on stored on digital devices
such as a computer's random
access memory, hard drives,
floppy drives, CDs, DVDs,
printers or other. Such
evidence is found in
mainframe computers,
minicomputers, PCs
laptops, notebooks,
tablet PCs, organizers, PDAs

Collage of Memory Cards

and other devices. Clearly, there are other devices besides
computers where digital evidence may exist. The pictures in
a digital camera may be evidence -- as could be the pictures
or phone numbers in a cellular phone or the scanned
information in a fax machine or scanner.

There's a dizzying array of memory types for cameras,
PDAs, etc. Of the many digital devices in use today, any
could contain evidence required in an investigation. It seems
certain, too, that the future will bring us many more

digital devices that are presently unimagined. Any of these, now or in the future, could be the subject of a computer forensics investigation.

Digital evidence can be thought of as being divided into either of two types: direct evidence or operational evidence.

Direct Evidence

DIRECT EVIDENCE

- **Letters**
- **Lists**
- **Financial data**
- **Spreadsheets**
- **Documents**
- **Logs and diaries**
- **Web pages**
- **Databases**
- **Email**
- **Graphics**
- **Audio**
- **Video**
- **Computer Programs**
- **Email address book**

Direct Evidence is created, downloaded, copied or otherwise acquired by the user of the digital device or computer. It is evidence that he or she is aware of and has taken some purposeful steps to create or acquire and to store and maintain.

Examples of evidence that fall into the direct category include: databases, email, graphics, audio, video, some computer programs, address books, letters, lists, financial data, spreadsheets, documents, logs, diaries, financial reports, personnel records and personal phone numbers. Direct evidence that has been found on criminals' seized computers has included drug dealers' transaction ledgers, pornographic online ads, graphics for counterfeit bills, forged cashier's checks, forged certificates, online ads for fraud schemes, email to/from co-conspirators, To-Do lists for crimes and many more.

Operational Evidence

The second category of evidence to be found on computers is Operational Evidence, evidence that is created by or placed there by the computer's operating system or application software. Operational evidence is produced or maintained by the computer for the proper operation of the system or for the convenience of the user. Operational evidence can be changed or deleted but it's difficult to do so. Users usually either don't know the evidence is there or they don't know how to hide, change or get rid of it. Most people don't know that a computer keeps a record of system events, or that web browsers dutifully record a history of internet sites visited. Most people don't know that the computer's print buffers contain pages of information even after printing is complete, or that many websites place a record right on your computer of your visit to their site.

OPERATIONAL EVIDENCE

- **MAC Times**
- **System Logs**
- **Registry**
- **Cache Files**
  - **Favorites**
  - **Recent**
  - **History**
  - **Cookies**
- **MetaData**

Computer operating systems such as Windows usually maintain logs containing administrative data plus information regarding events that occur during processing. Such logs often contain the user's name, time of logon or power up, and the time of last use. They might even contain a record of installation and execution of particular programs -- that information reveals a computer user's activities and may even suggest the intent of the user at a particular time.

MAC times are dates and times that the system logs with almost every system event that occurs. MAC is an acronym that derives from Modified, Accessed, Created. These events are logged in a file's directory, an index maintained to help the system locate the file. Events such as: this file was created at such and such a time, or this file was just modified, or just accessed are all logged.

Other events that are logged by the system and stamped with date/time would include such things as when a certain web page is downloaded and viewed, when a particular user logged on or off the computer, when the computer was started or stopped, etc. There are hundreds of such events that are logged and date/time stamped by the computer system or by application programs.

Metadata is information about a file that is stored within the file by the system software or by a native application (such as Microsoft Word or Microsoft Excel). Metadata may not be normally, or even easily, available to view by the user. Metadata could include such information as date and time of file creation, or of file modification or of any other event that occurs relative to a file. It could include the name of the computer in which the file resides, or information about the location of the file on the computer.

Microsoft Word metadata normally logs within the file a large amount of information about the file and about the user. For example, it logs the name of the person who is logged onto the computer and using the application; it logs the date/time of use, and how long the application has been used cumulatively. It even tries to log the ten most recent users who have edited the file and where the file was located during each such use. Most Metadata can be accessed and/or removed through the use of standard (or sometimes by special) software for the purpose.

Generally, much of the information we have been discussing in this section of the book, both direct and operational evidence, remains on the computer even after diligent attempts to erase or destroy it. And if it is there, a computer forensic examination will find it.

Email Evidence

Email is often an important source of direct evidence. Both Netscape and Internet Explorer, two well-known Internet browsers, archive email messages in their own files and folders. Both have elaborate facilities for cataloging received and sent messages. They even archive deleted emails. Most email software offers such features.

Old email messages can be found not only in a browser's dedicated email files and folders but also in unused disk space. That's because in processing and accessing email, copies of messages are placed in temporary files and can remain on the disk long after the message is read and discarded and long after the temporary file is deleted.

On some networking systems, each person's email is stored on the server and thus may not exist long on a user's workstation. In such systems, old email is purged from the server at regular intervals. In these cases, old email messages may be found on the server's backup tapes.

Another email service that's popular is web-based email that's stored and accessed on the Internet via a web browser. Copies of old email may possibly be found on the user's PC in unused disk space even though it comes from a web-based email server. As in the case of local area networked systems where email is stored on the server, copies of old email from web-based systems may have to be obtained from server backup tapes. If the server belongs to an Internet Service Provider (ISP), obtaining copies of old email could, possibly require a subpoena.

Tracing the source of Internet-borne email messages can pose problems for the computer forensics expert. Each computer has an address assigned to it that uniquely identifies that computer at a given time. These are called IP Addresses. Sometimes the originator's IP address appears with an email message but this is too often not the case. Further, the source information of many email messages is spoofed (purposely changed to mislead the recipient and investigators). It is still sometimes possible to trace these messages back to their origin but this can be a complicated process.

Where Evidence is Found

Evidence on a disk drive may exist as a normal file in the disk's data area or as a deleted file or fragment in unallocated (unused) space or in file slack (see the Appendix for definitions). Normal files are the currency of any computer's file system. File systems are that part of a computer's operating system responsible for managing files on the computer's floppy drives, hard drives and other devices. Some file systems include the FAT File System used in Windows 9x operating systems, the NTFS File System used in Windows NT, 2000 and XP Operating Systems and the TxF File System of Windows Vista. File systems differ but their concept of operation is about the same regardless of which one is used so they need concern us no further in this introductory treatment of computer forensics.

DIRECT EVIDENCE FOUND IN:

- Normal files
- Recycle Bin
- Deleted files
- File fragments
- Swap file
- Virtual memory
- Temporary files
- Unallocated space
- File slack
- Printer Spool
- FAX buffer
- Other

In many cases, whole files or fragments of files that have been deleted can be recovered. When files are first "deleted" in a Windows system, they are not actually deleted; rather, they are only marked for deletion -- but are moved to the Recycle Bin where they are indexed. A file indexed in the Recycle Bin can usually be recovered intact.

Files or fragments that have been deleted from the Recycle Bin may still be found in unallocated space or in file slack (see Appendix for definitions). When a file is finally deleted from the Recycle Bin, its data remains unchanged until another file needs its disk space. Once overwritten by another file's data, the original file's data is no longer available for normal recovery. Even then, though, the deleted file may not have been completely overwritten and a fragment of it may remain to be found many months or even years later by the computer forensics expert. Deleted files and fragments often contain important evidence and there is specialized forensic software designed to search for them in all parts of a disk including unallocated space and file slack.

Many applications, and perhaps even the operating system, spread pieces of files and file fragments throughout a computer's disk. That's because during processing of a user's data, many computer programs create temporary files that also contain the user's data. Temporary files aid the application in its processing tasks. When the application program is finished, it normally deletes its temporary files. However, the data in these files continues to occupy disk space until that space is needed by another file -- just as does the data from any deleted file. And even though the directory index of the original file may long since have passed from the disk, the entire temporary file or fragments of it may remain there for months or years.

It also sometimes happens that a computer program ends abnormally and is unable to delete all of its temporary files. In that case, even though a user may somehow destroy his original evidence file, that same evidence may remain on the disk as a temporary file to be found later by the computer forensics investigator.

The Swap File is a Windows system's virtual memory. It is used to temporarily store information for which there may be no room in the computer's random access memory (RAM). The swap file may not contain normal files exactly,

INTRODUCTION TO COMPUTER FORENSICS

but it could contain temporary copies of the same data that is or has been part of a normal file. The contents of the Swap File is always examined for evidence during a computer forensics investigation.

The operating system's Registry, a sort of system filing cabinet, is a place where the operating system, application programs and visited websites store or access information needed to conduct their activities on the computer. Much evidence concerning a user's computer activities are available in the Registry.

Internet cache files are files maintained by the computer system when a user browses the internet. They log which websites are viewed by a user, which files are downloaded -- and log entries usually include a time/date stamp. They may even store a copy of the actual web page that was viewed. Cache files are usually organized in categories and can reveal to us such information as which sites are a user's favorite, which were viewed most recently, which were viewed last week or the week before. Some sites even place what are called *cookies* on the user's computer. A cookie is a small customer record that a website accesses whenever the user logs onto that site.

Metadata refers to extra information that is attached to a file that a user creates. For example, when the word processor MS WORD is used to create a letter or other document, WORD takes information from the operating system, information such as the user's logon name, and copies that into the file being created. Metadata is updated each time the user opens the file or edits the file. It also records many other events. Metadata can be a rich source of information for a computer forensics expert.

The printer spool or buffer (where files temporarily await printing) may also contain evidence. FAX machines and other devices buffer data too and they may contain evidence of interest. There are other places where evidence is found but the space limitation of this book does not permit each to be covered.

A thorough and innovative computer forensics expert will find the evidence wherever it exists.

Hard Drive Capacity

The size of modern disk drives is a serious obstacle to the recovery and collection of evidence from computers. Even if the evidence is neither protecte d by passwords, hidden, encrypted or booby-trapped, the job of the computer forensics examiner is made difficult by the sheer size of modern digital storage. Hard drive capacity increases every year and has now grown to where it is clearly impractical for humans to visually search a modern hard drive.

It's difficult to really comprehend the capacity of modern disk drives. Here are some facts that may help. The most commonly installed hard drives today are very large; a 300 GB hard drive would be considered small. Nevertheless, a hard drive that's only 300 GB can contain: as many letters (a few hundred billion) as there are stars in our Milky Way

Galaxy, or as there are galaxies in our known universe (give or take a factor of two).

A 300 GB hard drive can store the equivalent of more than forty-five million single-spaced, typed sheets. This would be a stack of paper 15,000 feet high – that's a almost three miles. Or, it could store about two hundred and twenty-five thousand average hardcover novels (Michael Crighton's 360-page novel *Prey* is a good example). Stacked in the normal way, that pile of novels would rise to a height of almost five miles.

Imagine trying to search all the data that could be stored on such a hard drive. We have powerful software to help us in the search and we continue to develop better, faster software and better, faster techniques so that we may search smarter. Never-the-less, the capacity of computer storage devices is going to continue to grow for the indefinite future. Will we be able to keep up? We think so.

Chapter

4

Computer Forensics Cases II

Ex-Boyfriend Installs Key-Logger

In early 2003 in a suburb of Los Angeles a young woman finds files missing from her computer. She has reason to believe that an ex-boyfriend, a software engineer, has been coming into her house while she is at work and, as she says, "doing things to her computer." She's scared; she feels she's being stalked by this guy.

She hires an IT Security expert to examine her computer and to install a hidden motion activated camera near her computer at home. He does so. He also installs security software on her computer, hoping to prevent unauthorized access.

A week later, the camera snaps images of someone moving about the room at a time when the woman was at work – the intruder's face cannot be clearly seen on the film. Nevertheless, the woman believes the images are of her ex-boyfriend. Others are not so sure. In spite of this lack of certainty, the woman files a criminal complaint against the ex-boyfriend and petitions the court for a restraining order. A judge grants the restraining order.

The IT Security expert again examines her computer and finds that since the time he had been there the week before, the security software he had installed has been disabled. He also finds that new software has been installed on her computer. The new software includes a key-logger program and a program that would enable access to all her files by someone logging onto her computer via the Internet[2].

A few days later the police stop the ex-boyfriend's car a half a block from her house. In the car they find burglary tools and his laptop computer. The boyfriend is arrested and his computer seized and sent to the law enforcement computer forensics unit where a thorough examination of the laptop is conducted. Along with other evidence a copy of the same key-logger program and a copy of the Trojan, the Internet access program that had been installed on the woman's home computer, are found to be resident on the ex's laptop. He claims total innocence of the crimes, insisting that he uses these programs in his work.

At trial the jury does not believe the ex-boyfriend. He is found guilty and sentenced to five years.

A Stalking in Virginia

Here's an example of a crime In Virginia whose solution was aided by direct evidence. The diary shown below was found on the bad guy's computer.

---

[2] *This software is known as a Trojan or Trojan Horse (from the Trojan War) because it is sometimes introduced into the computer in a form that is not what it seems.*

INTRODUCTION TO COMPUTER FORENSICS

The culprit kept a chilling computer diary of his crimes. He stalked a woman for over a year, dutifully logging his stalking exploits in his computer diary. At the end of his diary he wrote that if he couldn't have this woman, nobody would.

PERSONAL DIARY ON COMPUTER

4-29-99 *I spoke to her at the market. She turned her back on me.*

5-15-99 *I rang her doorbell. Her roommate answered so I left.*

6-1-99 *I phoned again. She hung up on me.*

6-2-99 *I waited outside her apartment. I saw her leave with same guy again.*

6-10-99 *She answered the door this time. She yelled at me so I ran away.*

6-12-99 I waited outside again. *She came out with HIM again. They drove away.*

6-13-99 *IF I CAN'T HAVE HER NOBODY WILL.*

Then he killed her. Need I say, when his computer was searched by a computer forensics expert, his "Dear Diary" days were over.

Identity Theft Ring

Police in California recently busted a well-organized identity theft ring, a group of about half a dozen men and women. Their crimes were planned with great care and with hardly a detail omitted. They'd steal mail from mailboxes hoping to get information about a person. When they did, they'd use their computer to create various forms of ID – these would include counterfeit birth certificates and other bogus documents. Armed with a social security number and their fake IDs, they'd apply to the State of California for an interim driver's license. At this point they could apply for credit cards in the victim's name.

They'd use the credit cards to make large purchases. To enable them to continue to use the credit cards as long as possible, they would even make the credit card payments for a few months on purchases they had made.

For a long time, even though citizens had been complaining about ID theft to authorities in the area, law enforcement had no knowledge of the gang or of its connection with the thefts. Then something coincidental and totally unexpected happened: one member of the ring was arrested for some minor crime not connected with Identity theft. Police searched his house and seized his computer.

On that computer they found an amazing amount of direct evidence: a list showing the names, addresses and phone numbers of gang members; a list of more than fifty victims; images of counterfeit checks and fake IDs; credit card payment schedules and many other incriminating documents. Perhaps most surprising, they found what, if it had existed in a corporation, could only be called a Policies and Procedures Manual, written instructions on how to conduct every part of their nefarious business.

Needless to say, that identity theft ring is kaput.

MAC Times Solve Murder

Here's a crime that was solved by using a computer's MAC times – operational evidence that identified and nailed a suspect. In the Midwest, an entire family was murdered. At first, authorities were at a loss to find either a motive or a suspect. Then, on the family's old Atari computer, computer forensics experts found a letter dated several weeks before the murders.

The letter was supposedly written by the father in the murdered family. It granted valuable stock options to an employee. Computer forensics experts, using the computer system's MAC times, were easily able to show that the letter was actually written within minutes after the murders. Apparently the killer murdered the entire family then calmly sat down at their computer and composed the bogus letter granting stock options to himself.

That employee wasn't free to collect his stock options.

Metadata Reveals BTK Killer

The BTK killer, a serial killer, had committed his killings in and around Wichita Kansas between 1974 and 1991 The term *BTK* had attached to the murderer soon after the first several killings; it stood for *Bind, Torture, Kill* -- as a appropriate to the compassionless, savage and heinous nature of each of the killings. The media thought the appellation, BTK, was fitting and aptly nailed the murderer's M.O. (modus operandi). As of January of 2004, the thirtieth anniversary of the first of his killings, BTK had been neither identified nor caught. He had committed ten known murders;

five in 1974, two in 1977, one in each of 1978 and 1979, and a final one in 1991. An attempted murder in 1979 was also attributed to him. The thirtieth anniversary of his first killings spawned renewed interest in the BTK case.

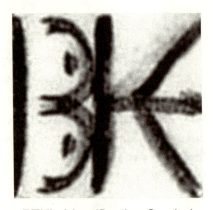

BTK's Identification Symbol

In January of 2004 a Local newspaper, the Wichita Eagle, published an article about the old and nearly forgotten case. The paper announced that a new book about the case would be published that year. As it turned out, BTK still lived and worked in Wichita and he read about himself in the newspaper. Apparently unwilling to let someone else tell his story, he began communicating: first with the news media then later, directly with law enforcement.

In March of that year he mailed an envelope to the Wichita Eagle. The return address on the envelope was <u>B</u>ill <u>T</u>homas <u>K</u>illman and the envelope contained copies of trophies that he had been saving for thirty years: Xerox copies of three photos of one of his female victims, a Xerox of her driver's license and a letter that included his well-known BTK symbol from the years of his crimes.

Within a few weeks, BTK mailed another letter to KAKE-TV; it was a puzzle of words and numbers arranged in columns. Again BTK verified the letter's authenticity by including his unique symbol. Only later was the puzzle deciphered. The third letter came a month later in the form of a package taped to a stop sign in Wichita. Inside was another of BTK's cruel taunts: a cartoon-like sketch of the victim of one of his murders that included a confusing but crude caption. Most interesting though, BTK had included an outlined Table of Contents for a possible book of his own about his crimes. He called the first chapter in his outline, *A Serial Killer is Born.* At the time, no one could figure out how he planned to publish a book about *his* crimes without revealing himself. They would soon find out.

The FBI worked along with the Wichita Police during each step of these events. Law enforcement officers were concerned that some careless move by them or by the media might cause BTK to start killing again. Wichita police and the FBI could tell that BTK's desire to communicate with them was driven by his ego and they concluded that he was probably proud of what he had done; they tried to keep him communicating, hoping he would make a misstep along the way.

The media, too, recognized the danger that their stories in the news might incite the killer anew. Police had asked them to withhold certain information regarding what was included in BTK's

I have spotted a female that I think lives alone and/or spotted a latchkey kid. Just got to work out the details. I'm much older (not feeble) now and have to condition myself carefully. Also my thinking process is not as sharp as it used to be ... I think fall or winter would be just about right for the HIT. Got to do it this year or next! ... time is running out for me.

BTK's Message

communications and packages and they complied. In the middle of July a worker at the Wichita Public Library found yet another BTK package that had been slipped through the book return slot. This one included a message challenging police by suggesting that BTK was again trolling for victims. Needless to say, this message caused great terror in the hearts of those who knew about it.

After this disturbing note there was a brief hiatus. Then in October a worker at UPS found a manila envelope in a UPS box. With this package, BTK seemed to be once more suggesting to police that he was about to start killing again. The envelope contained cards with pasted on images of children. BTK had drawn what seemed intended to represent bindings on the faces and bodies of the children. He also enclosed his autobiography in which he claimed his father had died in the war. It identified men his mother had dated and it said he loved trains and in fact lived near the railroad yard. He also included the year of his birth: 1939. This autobiography was published in the newspapers a few weeks later. Police assumed the whole thing was produced by BTK as an attempt to mislead them.

In December a new package from BTK was found leaning against a tree in a local park. Inside was a child's doll with hands and feet bound in such a way as to mimic one of BTK's murders. The missing driver's license of one of his victims, one killed in 1977, was also enclosed. This package, it was later learned, had been found just a few weeks before BTK became the latest president of the Congregational Council at his church in Wichita; he had been the council's vice president during 2004 and was automatically elevated to president on the first day of 2005. Naturally, no one else at the church (or anywhere else for that matter) knew their new council president was the BTK killer.

Eight days later, BTK packed another submission for Wichita law enforcement: a Special K cereal box. He filled it with more information concerning not only some of his murders and but also concerning some of his actual or potential victims – people he had stalked. In this box he also placed more misleading information about himself and his home. He warned police that his house in Wichita (which he said was three-storied and had an elevator) was alarmed and armed. He said a bomb in the basement would explode if police broke in. He marked the box with the words "BTK" and "bomb" and left it in the bed of a pickup truck in the parking lot of a Home Depot Store. An employee of the store, on his way home that evening, noticed the box in his truck but thought someone had tossed it there as trash. When he arrived home he put the box in the garbage can.

It was a few days before the employee realized what that Special K box could be; when he did, the box was still in his garbage can. He called police. Surveillance cameras from the Home Depot

Can I communicate with Floppy and not be traced to a computer. Be honest. Under Miscellaneous Section 494, (Rex, it will be OK). Run it for a few days in case I'm out of town-etc. I will try a floppy for a test run some time in the near future-February or March.

BTK's Note

parking lot for January eighth showed a man in a black Jeep Cherokee putting something in the employee's truck. The camera was too far from the scene to clearly show the face of the man in the Cherokee. By measuring the wheel base of the vehicle on the surveillance tape, police were able to clearly identify details of the Cherokee including the model year. Allowing himself to be seen on a surveillance camera was BTK's *second* mistake.

His *first* mistake involved something he had included in the package he left in the Home Depot employee's truck – and that mistake would

Thank you for your quick response on #7 and 8. Thank to the news team for their efforts. Sorry about Susan's and Jeff's colds.
Tell WPD that I receive Newspaper Tip for a go. Test run soon. Thanks.
PS: May want to use KTV-PC-etc code # and Letters from me for my Verification code to you.

BTK's Postcard

take several more iterations of BTK's story to play out.

With the package he had enclosed a note to police asking if he could in the future communicate with them via a computer diskette. This is what he wanted to know: if he put his communications to them on a computer diskette would they would be able to locate the computer from which it came. He directed that the cops could provide him the answer by placing an ad in the Miscellaneous Section of the Wichita Eagle Newspaper using the code name "Rex." Apparently BTK had heard of computer forensics but amazingly posed his lethal question to the very people who were on a life or death quest to catch him. Go figure! But then, BTK had never heard of metadata.

On the appointed day the FBI ad appeared. As almost anyone (except, of course, BTK) would have known in advance that it would, it did reassure him -- saying simply "Rex, it will be OK."

Toward the end of January another cereal box (Post Toasties this time) was found. This was the second cereal box from BTK. Get it? Cereal box, *Cereal* Killer! The package looked as though it had been in the weather for a while. It contained more cruel mementos of BTK's crimes. Then at the start of February a postcard arrived from BTK. It read as shown above with grammatical and spelling errors and all. BTK was trying to be folksy, he was now a "pal" of law enforcement. He acted almost as if he thought he was one of them. In the postcard he made reference to the ad (*"Rex it will be OK"*) the Wichita police and the FBI had put in the Wichita Eagle.

The receipt of this card excited the Wichita Police and the FBI; they almost couldn't believe their luck. They didn't have to wait long either. Before two weeks had passed, another package arrived. This time it was addressed to the television station KSAS-TV in Wichita and in it was an item of jewelry, a letter -- and the prize: the eagerly anticipated floppy diskette. BTK had apparently believed the detectives when they assured him via their posting in the Wichita Eagle newspaper that there could be no way, using the floppy, that they could identify him.

Law enforcement computer forensics investigators immediately conducted an examination of the diskette. On it they found a file that contained a Microsoft WORD document. Metadata in the document identified a particular church in Wichita and gave a man's first name as the "Author" of the document. A simple Internet search quickly produced not only the location of the church but a list of the first and last names of officers of the Church Congregational Council. The Congregational Council's President was listed and had the same first name as the author of the Microsoft WORD document on the floppy diskette. It was not difficult for law enforcement officers to find the address of this man.

Police drove by the man's house and noticed a black Jeep Cherokee in the driveway. The model year of the Jeep was the same model and year as the one seen on surveillance cameras in the Home Depot parking lot. Police were almost certain that they had the right man but they needed proof. That proof they obtained by subpoenaing DNA from the medical records of a member of the man's family and comparing it to the killer's DNA taken from the bodies of some of the victims. The DNA analysis proved the family member was related to the killer. Law enforcement had their man -- thanks to a lot of persistent and dedicated police work and to Microsoft WORD's metadata.

The Congregational Council President was easily arrested and confessed to the ten killings. In his confession he told detectives that, in addition to the ten murders, in the 1980s and 1990s he had stalked two women but had failed to complete the two "projects," as he called them. Both intended victims had filed restraining orders against him. One also moved away. BTK further admitted in his interrogators that he had planned to kill again and had set a deadline for his next killing "project," had identified his victim and had been stalking her.

He was tried and convicted and is serving ten life sentences (Kansas did not have the death penalty at the time the crimes were committed). He will be eligible for parole from the Kansas State Prison System in February of the year 2180.

The BTK killer will be over two hundred years old then.

Microsoft's Email Troubles

A few years ago the Justice Department sued Microsoft for antitrust violations. They charged that Microsoft tried to illegally extend its monopoly over the PC Operating System market by forcing vendors to use Internet Explorer for their default Internet browser. During discovery on that case a series of emails between Microsoft executives turned up among the tens of thousands on Microsoft's network servers.

In one email a Microsoft executive wrote: "Getting Apple to do anything that significantly/materially disadvantages Netscape will be tough." A high level executive was said to have written emails to a half-dozen key executives. That email said: "Do we have a clear plan on what we want Apple to do to undermine Netscape?"

Microsoft lost the suit and these emails were instrumental in proving the charges against Microsoft.

The Sniper Case

John Allen Muhammad and Lee Boyd Malvo shot at least 18 people in 2002. Their case became known as the "sniper" case.

The two killers had removed the rear seat of their car and otherwise modified it so that they could lie down in the trunk and, with the lid down, fire their rifle from inside the car at victims a long distance away. During their murder spree, the nation was in terror. One man was killed at a gas station while putting gas in his car. Another person, a woman, died instantly in a mall parking lot when she was shot as she returned to her car. A bus driver was shot as he stepped from his bus, killed while enjoying a smoke on his break. And there were others. People were afraid to leave their houses even to go to work.

The killers were hunted and eventually apprehended but only after committing numerous murders of innocent individuals. Found with the two men in the car in which they were sleeping when they were caught was a Sony Laptop that was presumed to have been stolen from an earlier victim who they had killed during a robbery. On the laptop were carefully detailed maps with skull and crossbones marking the locations of their shootings. At one location on the map, a Home Depot where Linda Franklin was shot and killed from 160 yards away, the killers had annotated the skull and crossbones with the words "Good one."

The police also found a PDA organizer with the men that contained a list of names titled: "People to Die Later." Malvo has been sentenced to life in prison and Muhammad, the older of the two, has been sentenced to death. The digital contents of the laptop and the PDA were instrumental in convicting them.

Print Buffer Solves Bank Holdup

The demand note found at the scene of a bank robbery had been produced and printed on a computer and the police thought they knew who did it. They searched the suspect's home and seized his computer. The computer forensics examiner found no evidence of the demand note in the suspect's computer memory. Then he looked in the print buffer.

The culprit thought he had avoided leaving any trace of the note because he had never asked the computer to save it. To his way of thinking, since he had never asked the system to save the file, there should have been no record of it on the computer's disk drive. What he did not know, however, was that when he printed the note the system sent a copy of it to the printer's spool buffer where it remained until the computer forensic examiner found it – direct evidence of the suspect's guilt.

Where that culprit now lives there are no banks to be robbed.

Employee Surfs Web for Stolen Goods

An employee of a Southern Nevada electronics distributor, along with three of his pals, was stealing products from the company's warehouses. Stolen products included computers, cell phones, and other such items. In order to determine at what prices they should advertise these items on sites such as Ebay, the employee and his three friends would surf the web to find out what others were asking for the same products. They would determine what prices legitimate (and other) sellers were charging for similar products and price theirs accordingly.

When company officials realized that large numbers of products from their inventory were disappearing at an alarming rate, they launched an investigation. They soon discovered the thieving employee and sent his company computer to a computer forensics investigator.

The investigator found suspicious email exchanges on the computers between the employee and members of his gang but there was nothing definitive, nothing that would prove the employee's guilt – nothing that is until the computer forensics guy got to the culprit's Internet surfing history. There, he found that there had been searches of web sites for the exact items that had been stolen. Those findings led him to saved computer files that contained copies of web pages featuring the stolen items. Again, not definite proof of guilt but enough with which to confront the employee.

The employee confessed his crimes, agreed to resign his position with the company, and worked with company executives to establish a long-term plan for making restitution. His accomplices in the scheme were never charged with any crime but the employee will be repaying the company with hard cash until the year 2026.

Chandra Levy Case

In another famous case it was not the suspect's intentions that were the subject of the computer forensics examination but those of the victim. And these intentions were uncovered as a result of the discovery on her home computer of operational evidence that appeared there because of the victim's search of the internet just before the Levy's murder.

Chandra Levy lived in Washington D.C. where she was an intern at the Bureau of Prisons and an aide to a then Member of the House of Representatives. Prior to that time she had lived with her parents in a small town in Northern California. She had been scheduled to leave for California on a short visit later on the day she disappeared, May 30, 2001. Because she had been having a liaison with a married Member of Congress, the case became national news. Extensive searches by many interested citizens in the Washington DC area failed to locate any sign of her. Psychics said her body would be found near "some trees down in a marshy area."

A computer forensics investigation of her computer at her Washington home showed that earlier on the day she disappeared she had written some emails, looked up some information regarding flights to California, and searched for a map to the Klingle Mansion in the 1700 acre Rock Creek Park near her residence. This information set off three intensive searches in that park. Nothing was found there at the time.

What may have seemed like a missing person case sadly turned out something much more macabre. Fifteen months after her disappearance, a man looking for turtles in Rock Creek Park discovered her skeleton in a steep, roughly wooded section of the park.

This is an example of how computer forensics can reveal not only a person's activities but also their intentions. The findings of computer forensics specialists, though not fully realized at first, in the end turned out to be correct. Authorities now know that Chandra Levy had gone running in the park, the same park mentioned in the original search of her computer. She had been accosted in the park and raped, then killed by a man who was a stranger to her.

The killer has since been identified, caught, tried and convicted. He is now serving a life sentence in prison.

Metadata Strikes Again

A project manager at a medium-sized computer consulting firm decided to accept a high level position at a competing firm. He turned in his notice and prepared to leave the original firm. During his final week he stayed late at the office on several nights so that he could copy company files onto three floppy disks that he planned to take with him to the new company. He convinced his secretary to aid him in the nighttime copying projects.

Among the records that he took from the original company were a half dozen proposals that he had personally prepared, proposals for contract s with potential clients that would have meant a great deal of income for his original consulting firm. These proposals included details of the respective projects, details of the work, how each would be completed, schedules for completion, inside costs, and proposed prices. In other words, complete workups on the projects, everything that would be needed to prepare for and conduct the work according to the client's requirements. These proposals had all been written on the project manager's desktop computer in Microsoft WORD – a well-known word processing system.

Once at the new company, minor modifications were made to the proposals to make them look as though they had originated with the new company; titles and headings were changed, some dates were updated, the names of the participants were changed, and the cover letters were copied almost without change to the new company's letterhead. The proposals were circulated by computer to other staff members at the new company who reviewed them and sometimes made minor edits. The proposals were then submitted to the potential clients.

Most of these activities by the former project manager were in violation of his contract and non-disclosure agreements with his original employer. Over a short period of time a majority of the contracts with these potential clients that resulted from this set of proposals were awarded to the project manager's new company.

The original company had lost a number of potential clients and millions in income. They felt they had been cheated so they sued the former employee and his new employer. Such cases can take time and this one was no exception. It was several years before the case came to trial. During this time, most of the contracted projects had been completed and during their execution many computer files had been produced: communications between the principals, schedules for completion, progress reports, materials orders, and others.

About two years in, during the discovery phase of the trial, the court ordered the new employer to produce all records that resulted from their work with the clients brought to them by the project manager. This they did. That production amounted to hundreds upon hundreds of computer files and thousands of pages of hardcopy documents.

Among the files that were part of this production were numerous Microsoft WORD files that contained metadata. Metadata in Microsoft WORD is not normally visible to one who view or edits the file normally. The metadata for any file can easily be obtained but many users do not even know it exists and so do not look for it. The metadata in some of these files showed clearly that the files were originated and edited at the project manager's original company.

Microsoft Word metadata often includes the logon usernames of the users on the last ten accounts that were opened while the file was being edited. It can also give the computer's path data for the file as it was edited. The metadata in some of these files of interest listed employees and computer file paths for the first few times the file was edited on the original company's computers. However, within the same file and in the same metadata output the names of employees at the new company appeared as having edited the files on their computers. Clearly, the files had been moved from the first company to the second.

This metadata proved that the files in question had originated at the project manager's original company. They had then been taken to the new company and subsequently used, with minor edits, by the new company to submit proposals to the clients.

Supporting these metadata conclusions were numerous hardcopies of documents that showed that the proposals as written at the original company had been submitted to the clients by the new company. The project manager and his new employer were found liable and were required to pay a large compensation to the original employer.

Once again, thanks to Microsoft WORD's revealing metadata.

GORDON PELTON

Chapter

5

Protected Computer Files

Although there are other methods used by those wishing to protect their computers or files from prying eyes, the most commonly used techniques involve passwords, encryption, or both.

Password Protection

Passwords are routinely used to prevent others from accessing our files or computers. Many features of the computer can be protected with passwords: the startup operation, logon to the operating system, exit from the screensaver, access to files, and others. In recent years, more and more robust password protection has evolved – though much software on the market today continues to provide only weak password protection. Even some of the weaker password schemes can be strengthened if the user chooses his or her passwords with care. In general, the longer a password, the greater the variety of special characters it contains and the less like common words, the harder it is to crack.

> **Guilty People:**
>
> ..... try to destroy email and other computer evidence they don't want us to see.

Regardless of whether or not the protection is effective, the computer forensics expert in many investigations must crack one or more passwords to gain access to computer evidence. The easiest and fastest method an investigator has of acquiring a computer password is to simply ask the computer's owner for it. If that doesn't work, the next most effective technique is to try the words written on scraps of paper found taped to the computer, under the keyboard or in the Rolodex.

Many times both of those approaches fail. But a number of manual password cracking techniques have evolved and are often easily applied by a knowledgeable

> **Guilty people also try to:**
>
> - **Delete it**
> - **Hide it**
> - **Booby-trap it**
> - **Use passwords**
> - **Encrypt it**
> - **Obscure it**
>
> **..... But we still find it!**

expert. Finally, we can let the computer help us find

passwords. Some very effective password-cracking software has been developed to aid us in these efforts. Some of this software actually searches the culprit's own hard drives and compiles a file of the words found there to try as passwords. It's amazing how often this approach yields results.

Encryption

For criminals and others who are looking to thwart investigation of their computer or files, encryption provides an inexpensive yet effective means. Encryption is a process that codes a file in such a way that a visual inspection of the file produces something that looks only like gibberish. To see the plaintext (the actual, readable content of the file) one is required to decrypt the file.

Decryption requires a key, the key that was used to encrypt the file – and, as with passwords, the key is protected by the file's owner. Once an investigator knows the encryption key, it is usually not a complicated matter for him or her to decrypt the file and reveal its contents.

ENCRYPTION: THE GOOD NEWS

- IT RAISES INVESTIGATOR'S CURIOSITY
- IT CAN BE SOMETIMES BE DECRYPTED
- INTENTIONAL HIDING CAN BE EVIDENCE OF GUILT

An encryption key is generally a string of characters that can be typed on a computer's keyboard. The key could be something simple like your mother-in-law's first name, the name of your favorite movie, or the first letters of every word in a poem. Amazingly, more than one criminal has been caught and convicted who used the encryption key shown on the next line of this book.

"Encrypted"

Usually, though, encryption keys are longer and more complex. They may be constructed from some formula, from a novel, from a phonebook, from the lyrics to a song or from any other writing known only to the user. For example, one encryption key was found to consist of the first letters of every word to the American Pledge of Allegiance.

Just as in the case of passwords, computer forensics experts must often crack encryption keys. This is done in a variety of ways, many of which are similar to those used for cracking passwords. The expert will ask the computer's user for the required keys. He will also search the user's work area for notes, clues and even for a copy of the key itself.

Sometimes the computer forensics investigator is rewarded in such a search. But sometimes,

FIND ENCRYPTION KEY

- **Ask user for key**
- **Search work area**
- **Try to guess the key**
- **Search user's files**
- **Try decryption software**

the same file that is encrypted can be found in plaintext either on the computer or on a floppy or other media. Plaintext is the target of a successful decryption of an encrypted file. More than once an investigator has found the plaintext version of the encrypted file somewhere on or near the computer. Obviously, finding the evidence elsewhere in plaintext avoids the need to decrypt a file; for an investigator, finding the plaintext is like finding the gold at the end of a rainbow.

Some computer forensics investigators can employ powerful software to help crack encryption keys. But often encryption is very difficult to crack and experts are frequently not successful in their efforts. Government law enforcement agencies have access to large budgets and sometimes find it necessary to employ the world's largest, fastest computers in their attempts to crack encryption. Even with these means their cracking software can require hours, days or even months attempting to crack the toughest keys.

Still, nothing is perfect. Often, even after the best efforts, these techniques and software packages do not find the required encryption key (or even a password) in the time available, particularly if the user has chosen well his password or key.

Many computer forensics experts have become quiet adept at bypassing a criminal's password or encryption schemes. One such approach involves deceiving the native software (the program that will open a file for the user once a correct password is provided). Depending on which native application program is involved, it may be possible to trick that program into believing that no password is required.

Chapter

6

Computer Forensics Cases III

<u>RIAA and File-Sharing</u>

Not too many years ago the Recording Industry Association of America (RIAA) was prosecuting people for sharing copyrighted music with unlicensed individuals. The process was generally referred to as "file-sharing" and computer software was available that facilitated these sharing activities via the Internet. A sharer could log onto a website, upload a list of songs resident on their computer that they were willing to share, and download the songs to other people's computers – all at small or no cost.

It was not always easy (and sometimes not possible) for RIAA investigators to learn who was doing the file downloading. They were easily able to themselves enter into the sharing transactions by logging onto the file-sharing websites, perusing the catalogs of songs available for downloading, and requesting that the songs be downloaded. Often the RIAA could tell who was offering songs to be downloaded from their computers because such information would be available on the website.

Typically, when someone logs onto the Internet and onto a website, they go through an Internet Service Provider (ISP). There are now and there were then numerous ISPs.

The ISP is often the only entity that is able to identify the user connecting to their website – and often even they cannot do that. For the RIAA to get access to that information they would generally be required to obtain a court order. But interested parties (e.g. the parties on the connection) could fight in court to prevent a court order from being issued. So, nothing about the job the RIAA had taken on was necessarily a slam dunk.

When the RIAA did know who was offering copyrighted songs for download without paying the proper license fee, they could subpoena the individual's computer and subject it to forensic analysis. There are a number of ways in which RIAA could demonstrate the guilt of someone. One would be if the ISP confirmed that the Internet connection did occur at the prescribed time and between the accused parties. Generally they would also have to demonstrate that the downloading had occurred. This could be done in several ways too. Often, the computer that was the target of the downloads would contain unlicensed copies of the songs in question. Often too, the Internet History (operational evidence) on the computer would demonstrate the connection or even the ongoing activities.

On more than one occasion the RIAA was able to find other evidence on the downloader's computer, evidence such as chat logs or emails between friends in which the downloading activities were described or discussed in great detail. Discovery of this kind of evidence would often be enough for the downloader to admit his or her crimes.

A Gambling Operation Busted

Operating in three California counties, a bookmaking ring managed their gambling records on a networked computer system. These records included the gang's daily take, their payables, their receivables etc. The records also included the names, addresses and phone numbers of bettors along with amounts bet and amounts won and lost.

The gang used a password to limit access to their records. When the gang was arrested, they refused to cooperate with law enforcement; they refused to give up the passwords. Police turned to the manufacturer of the accounting software used by the gang hoping they would help unlock the records. That company too refused to help.

Using procedures well-known to computer forensics practitioners, the computer forensics expert called in by police was able to get all the records. He eliminated the need for the password using forensic software to nullify it in the accounting program[3]. Thus was opened a four-year trove of information: the daily take on bets, client list, payables, receivables, and more.

The result: guilty pleas and a large payment of back taxes to both California and to the U.S. Treasury.

---

[3] *This involved tricking the accounting software into thinking no password was required for entry.*

Decrypted Files Reveal Terrorist Plot

When Ramsey Yousef was arrested, police found encrypted files on his laptop computer. Yousef was a member of the international terrorist group responsible for the first World Trade Center bombing in 1993 and for the bombing of a Manila airliner in 1995. The encrypted files on Yousef's computer were decrypted and found to contain plans for further destruction -- in particular, plans to blow up eleven U.S. airliners in flight in the Far East.

The plan was grounded.

Ifyoucanreadthisyoumustbeme

One computer hacker who was arrested for his crimes aided investigators examining his computer by voluntarily revealing his amusing encryption key. It was:

ifyoucanreadthisyoumustbeme--**oragoodcyberpunk.

Nobody would have ever guessed that.

Oh, What's Your Encryption Key?

Another hacker stealing credit card numbers was caught in a law enforcement sting. Thinking he had sold the numbers to another criminal, he willingly revealed the encryption key for the card number file to undercover cops.

The key had been constructed by concatenating the first several letters of each sentence in the first paragraph on page 128 of Mario Puzo's novel *The Last Don.*

Nobody would have ever guessed that either.

FBI Catches Spy, Aldrich Ames

After much effort, the FBI identified and arrested the CIA spy, Aldrich Ames. Ames had spent years passing the Untied States of America's national secrets to the Russians. A Russian agent operating as an officer in the Russian embassy in Washington D.C. picked up Ames' stolen documents from secret drops in parks and other areas around the city.

The FBI caught Ames red handed one night as he picked up one of the Russian payoffs from a drop under a bridge near his home. They seized his computers. After many hours, using specialized software and huge computers, the FBI was able to crack the encryption Ames used to protect secret files on one of his computers.

Turns out Ames had used his Russian code name, Kolokol, as the encryption key. The decrypted files provided key evidence in the case against him.

Florida's Secretary of State in 2002

Remember Florida's embattled Secretary of State during the 2000 presidential election? Recall that she was also Co-Chair of the "Florida for George Bush" campaign. In August

2001, led by the NY Times, a phalanx of newspapers pressured her to turn over four state-owned computers from her office for examination. They hoped to show that Republican operatives influenced what she told election officials about how to treat overseas absentee ballots. They also thought some election records may have been deleted.

Experts from a Minneapolis firm conducted a computer forensics examination on the four computers and allegedly reported that documents were found on one of the computers suggesting that the Secretary of State had been using state time and equipment for political activities. Apparently any violations that were found were of minor interest because, allegedly, these findings were subsequently largely ignored.

Of importance is the fact that the newspaper consortium concluded that their concerns were unfounded and that there was no reason to believe she had changed her position with respect to the treatment of absentee ballots. They also reported that, even though some files had been deleted, there was no evidence of wholesale intentional erasures.

This case is an example of a computer forensics examination reporting exculpatory results and essentially exonerating an accused.

Computer Forensics Gone Awry

Sometimes computer forensics findings can be misleading – and sometimes they can be just plain wrong. A few years ago I was called in on a case by an attorney whose client was being accused of a very serious crime by law enforcement officers and by the local district attorney. A critical piece of evidence against this unfortunate individual was a finding made by law enforcement's computer forensics investigator.

Police had seized this man's home computers (there was more than one) and sent them to the police computer forensics laboratory for examination. Investigators there found that on one of the computers he had been surfing the Internet for information about this type of crime and that he had performed this search before he had been accused of the crime and even before he would have known such a crime had been committed. They further claimed that on the same day he had done a Google search for information about the punishment for this particular crime. They claimed that neither of these searches would have been executed had he not himself committed the crime. If these assertions were true, they did seem to indicate a guilty conscience. A trial date was set.

The man's attorney called me and asked me to verify law enforcement's computer forensics results. I reviewed the pertinent police and computer forensics reports. The police computer forensics findings were necessarily based upon some very technical, esoteric and complicated reasoning having to do with the ways that the man's computer software produced and saved that particular operational data.

I found that, in fact, there had been the Google search and the Internet surfing on the man's computer as reported by the law enforcement computer forensics investigator. I also found that the date these activities were conducted was different from that claimed by law enforcement's computer forensics investigator. He claimed the date of the searches preceded the date that the suspect was accused of the crime and before the man could even have know that such a crime had been committed. In actuality, a correct interpretation of the operational data proved that all the searches had been conducted after the man had been accused of the crime. Instead of these searches indicating a guilty mind, they indicated the man acted quite reasonably under the circumstances.

After being shown the correct interpretation of law enforcement's findings, the District Attorney went before the court and explained their mistake.

This case showed that it is always a good idea to double check everything.

Chapter

7

Hidden Computer Evidence

General

Users with something to hide sometimes go to great lengths to conceal direct evidence. Many, not knowing how hard it is to actually remove traces of a file from a computer

PC with Cover Removed

will fruitlessly instruct the system to delete files. More sophisticated users try other means to hide evidence, often by making it look like something different than what it is. Other times they try stashing it in places they think will not be searched. Users have also been known to booby-trap their computer or files so that an unwary investigator will himself trigger the destruction of the evidence when he comes snooping around.

Other means, as discussed in a previous chapter, is to use password protection or encryption. It takes a little longer for us to gain access but most often the password or encryption key is found and the evidence obtained.. Users have discovered other clever ways to hide or obscure the data they are trying to protect. Success in revealing

HOW EVIDENCE IS HIDDEN

- Files deleted
- Files hidden off-site
- Metadata deleted
- Disk defragmented
- Disk or files wiped
- Disk or files compressed
- Disk formatted
- Computer booby-trapped
- File given misleading name
- File extension changed
- File moved to system folder
- File password-protected
- Files or disk encrypted
- Files given 'Hidden' attribute
- Folder given 'Hidden' attribute
- System time/date changed
- File given misleading extension
- File in "ALT 255" folder
- File put in 'Hidden' partition
- Font color changed
- Data placed in HPA
- Files compressed or archived
- Computer booby-trapped
- Steganography hides file
- File moved off-site
- Combinations of the above

hidden or obscured data is generally good but the level of

success does depend upon the methods used by the culprits.

Users hide evidence by deleting files, changing a file or folder attribute to 'hidden', changing system date/time, using misleading file names, using misleading file extensions, hiding a user file in a systems folder, placing a file in 'hidden' partition, setting font color same as background, putting a file in the HPA (host protected area), embedding one file in another file, or moving the file offsite. There are other ways - - not every technique is listed here and I'm sure more are being devised even as you read these words. A few of the possible evidence-hiding techniques are discussed in the following sections.

Concealed in System Folder

A common technique is to move a file to a systems folder and change the name to one that makes the file seem as though it belongs there[4].

Some users compress the data within a file so it will be harder to recognize if an investigator takes a closer look. Figure 4-1 shows part of the contents of a systems folder on a Windows computer. It lists various files used by the Windows Operating System. One of the files listed (in bold here) does not belong. It is innocuously disguised only because the file name and extension has been changed to MOUSE.DRV so it looks like it fits in among the others. The size of the file is not unusual and the date/time of the file has been changed to fit in too. This name, MOUSE.DRV, is

---

[4] *For an example of this technique see the chapter on the Black Baron in this book.*

GORDON PELTON

typical of the kind of names commonly found in system folders.

Figure 4-2 shows a closer view of some of the contents of the systems folder of Figure 4-1. In Figure 4-2, the file *MOUSE.DRV* is easily seen as the third item down the list.

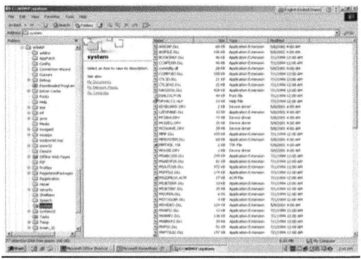

Figure 4-1   A Typical Windows System Folder

Figure 4-3 shows the actual contents of the disguised file *MOUSE.DRV*. The user has hidden a userid and a password there. In all probability this userid and password would enable us to open and read some other file that we would find on the same computer. Or, perhaps we would find the address of some website tucked away somewhere and *MOUSE.DRV* would provide access to that.

98

MMSYSTEM.DLL	68 KB	Application Extension	5/8/2001 4:00 AM
MMTASK.TSK	2 KB	TSK File	5/8/2001 4:00 AM
MOUSE.DRV	2 KB	Device driver	5/8/2001 4:00 AM
MSABC200.DLL	299 KB	Application Extension	7/1/1994 12:00 AM

Figure 4-2   Closer view of Figure 4-1

My client database:

UserID: Alexandra
Password: Rasputin

Figure 4-3   Contents of file *MOUSE.DRV*

By-the-way, this pair, <u>Alexandra</u> for the userid and <u>Rasputin</u> for the password, is not a good choice for anyone really wanting to protect their data from prying eyes. Passwords are protected but userids are not. Upon learning that the userid is Alexandra, anyone skilled in cracking passwords would immediately try for passwords the words <u>Russia</u>, <u>Nicholas</u>, and <u>Rasputin</u> in that order. It would take only ten seconds to crack this one.

Changed Font Color

Changing the color of a message's font is a convenient trick for hiding information. An email message that looks normal and straightforward and not at all suspicious can include additional words that are not normally visible to the casual reader. The hidden message can be made invisible to normal viewing software because if the writer of the message sets the font color of the hidden part identical to the background color. That trick makes the hidden part invisible to most email viewing programs.

However, on most email viewing software (but not all) the hidden line will stand out when highlighted. The hidden part can be revealed by anyone who knows the trick. By highlighting the entire page or pages on which the message is displayed the entire message will be rendered visible.

Steganography

The technique of hiding one file in another is called steganography. One dictionary defines steganography as: *"Hiding a secret message within another one in such a way that others cannot discern the presence or contents of the*

DEFINITION OF STEGANOGRAPHY

(FROM DICTIONARY.COM) HIDING A SECRET MESSAGE WITHIN A LARGER ONE IN SUCH A WAY THAT OTHERS CANNOT DISCERN THE PRESENCE OR CONTENTS OF THE HIDDEN MESSAGE.

hidden message." Steganography has been practiced for more than 2500 years. The term comes from the Ancient Greeks and originally meant *secret writing*. It is said that Osama Bin Laden and members of his al-Qaeda network have used steganography to exchange messages undetected over the Internet.

The story has been told of a messenger during the Persian Wars who shaved his head and had a message tattooed on his scalp. He waited until his hair grew back to make the journey and deliver his message. At his destination his head was shaved to reveal the message. Effective, but slow -- much slower than hiding the message in a picture file and emailing the picture as an attachment.

Figures 4-4 and 4-5 are near copies of the same photograph. One of the pictures has a 4000 letter message hidden within its file (that message is equivalent to about two pages of this book[5]). The pictures are identical except the computer data that represents one of them also contains all the data representing the text of the hidden four thousand word message. (It took about one minute for a computer program to merge the message into the picture.) Picture B of Figure 4-5 on the right contains the concealed message. The two pictures look almost exactly alike, don't they?

The original picture is represented in a file of about 42,000 bytes. Figure 4-5 with the message embedded in it has been increased by only one thousand bytes. You'd think the right-hand picture should be four thousand bytes longer than the original. But the way the message is embedded, it hardly increases the file's size. The computer bytes representing each letter in the message are broken up and merged into the picture's digital data in places that are of least importance to the picture. Thus, the visual changes to the picture with the hidden message are

---

[5] *See below for the text of the hidden message.*

Figure 4-4   Picture A   Figure 4-5   Picture B

minimal and the modified picture, while very slightly distorted, is hardly discernable from the original.

Steganographed images can be detected and their hidden messages extracted through the use of sophisticated software that performs statistical analyses of the image used as a container for the hidden message.

The message that is hidden in picture B of Figure 4-5 follows on this and the next two pages in italics. It is a short portion of a report by Stephen Lau of December 19, 2001 titled "An Analysis of Terrorist Groups' Potential Use of Electronic Steganography." It is important to note the length of the hidden message.

Abstract (a portion of the abstract)

The events of September 11th, 2001 have irrevocably altered the landscape of computer security. In the aftermath of these events, various urban legends and rumors have developed surrounding terrorists' online activities. One such topic has been in the alleged use of electronic steganography, a method to covertly hide messages within another, by terrorist groups. This paper provides an overview of steganography, its historical use during times of war, and how modern day electronic steganography can be accomplished. An overview is provided of current techniques to detect steganography on the Internet, which have so far failed to uncover any evidence of steganography on the Internet, and possible future avenues of research in detecting online steganography using techniques similar to the Federal Bureau of Investigation's Carnivore system. The paper concludes with examples of the dangers of unsubstantiated steganography claims and privacy considerations in detecting online electronic steganography.

The tragic events of September 11th, 2001 have caused a major reevaluation of security procedures within the United States. Overnight, seemingly normal events have become suspect. Potential terrorists and terrorist activity lurk in every aspect of United States life and culture. Although much of this increased awareness for security and of potentially suspicious activity is most likely an adverse short-term reaction to the September 11th events, it is obvious that many changes that have been set in motion since that date will be permanent. Fundamental changes in the approach to security both online and in real life are underway and will forever change our perceptions of both real life security and computer security.

Online criminal activity such as distributed denial of service attacks, web page defacements, cracker intrusions, are now perceived in a different light, especially by the mainstream American public. Long dismissed as being the online equivalent of teenage delinquency, they are now viewed as potential terrorist activity. An anti-terrorism bill, "USA Patriot Act"[24] recently enacted within the United States lists computer crimes such as web defacement and denial of service attacks as potential terrorist activity and subject to far more punitive damages than in the past. Government organizations, educational institutions and corporations are reviewing and removing or limiting access to information available on the Internet that can potentially be used for terrorist activity.

The capability of the Internet as a means of mass instant communication has helped to spread news and, unfortunately, rumors far and wide quite quickly. Instant urban legends appear almost daily. Not wanting to miss out on potential news stories, some of these rumors have been picked up by the United States mainstream media, giving it more "credibility" in the eyes of a large majority of the American public. This has lead to a confusing mix of both information and disinformation. Have you heard the story of the man who "surfed" the debris down from the 86th floor of the World Trade Center? A false story reported on many mainstream media sources.[25] How about the school kid in New York City who looked out the window in his classroom a week before September 11th and told his teachers that they wouldn't be there next week? Strangely enough, this "urban legend" was actually true. [26][1][1]

Sometimes Evidence is in Plain View

There have been many cases where a criminal, rather than making an effort to hide evidence, will actually shoot videos or write diary entries of the actual crimes he is committing and keep these stored on his computer. I suppose he thinks he will never be caught so it doesn't matter. Such cases make easy work for law enforcement and computer forensics investigators.

However, as discussed above, it happens often enough that criminals and others go to extraordinary lengths to hide what is on their computers; just as often, investigators must employ extraordinary means and a great deal of innovation to locate and extract hidden evidence.

Chapter

8

Destroyed Computer Evidence

There are as many ways to destroy evidence as there are people trying to do it. The usual means that people employ to destroy computer evidence are hardly ever completely successful. When there have been attempts to destroy evidence, we typically find that files have been deleted or disks have

A Computer Motherboard

been formatted, wiped or defragment. Some culprits booby-trap their computer to trigger one of the other methods in case an unauthorized access of their computer occurs. Each of these ways of destroying computer evidence is discussed in this chapter.

Deleted Files

DESTROYED EVIDENCE

- **Hidden Off-Site**
- **Deleted Files**
- **Defragmented Disk**
- **Wiped Disk or Files**
- **Compressed Files**
- **Formatted Disk**
- **Computer Booby-trapped**
- **Password-Protected**
- **Encrypted Files**
- **Hidden in Another File**
- **Combinations**

As has been suggested earlier, deleting a file in most operating systems on most computers does not actually delete the file. In a Windows system, for example, a deleted file is simply detached from its original folder (or directory) and reattached to the recycle bin. The recycle bin can be emptied at the discretion of a user. When the recycle bin is emptied, another step toward the actual destruction of the attached files is taken. However, that step still leaves files mostly intact – but they may not remain so.

When the recycle bin is emptied, the entry recording each file's assignment to the recycle bin remains on the disk but each is marked as being available for destruction. Files' data bytes also remain on the disk but the space they occupy is also marked as available for use by other files. Any deleted file or any part of it may be overwritten if a new file needs the disk space. Any part of a file that's overwritten is no longer recoverable. But what's important here is that the parts not overwritten can be recovered.

INTRODUCTION TO COMPUTER FORENSICS

Many people believe that deleting a file removes it permanently from the disk. Since this is not the case, much evidence from previously "deleted" files is later discovered either in the swap file, in unallocated space, in file slack or in all of them. Deleted files have turned around many a court case.

Formatted Disks

It often happens that someone who is trying to destroy evidence on their computer will format a disk drive thinking that all evidence is removed from the drive during the formatting process. In some cases of formatting, that actually does

HIDDEN EVIDENCE

- 'Hidden' Attribute on Files
- 'Hidden' Attribute on Folders
- Change System Time/Date
- Misleading File Names
- Misleading File Extensions
- Hide File in Sys Folder
- File in "ALT 255" Folder
- File in 'Hidden' Partition
- Font Color Synchronized
- Software That Hides Files
- Data Placed in HPA
- Compression/Archiving
- Steganography
- Hide File Off-Site
- Combinations of these

happen; the drive's data is overwritten and thus becomes unrecoverable. However, not all data is overwritten during formatting.

Operating systems each have their own way of formatting drives, whether they are floppies, hard drives, or other types of drives. Additionally, there can be more than one option available for formatting in any given situation. For example, on

> ## Deleted Files: The Good News
>
> - Recycle Bin Saves Files
> - Data may remain
> - Intentional destruction is evidence of guilt

Windows systems there are *quick* (or *partial*) and *full* format options available. If a full format is executed on a floppy under Windows 9x, all data areas on the floppy are overwritten making it impossible to recover any files from that floppy. However, a full format operation performed with the same operating system on a hard drive would not overwrite the drive's data area. Thus, the hard drive's data remains and though it may be difficult, that data can be recovered. Quick or partial formatting in Windows does not overwrite a disk's data.

Every drive maintains a record of its files in an index (called a directory) telling where the files' data are located on the drive. What typically happens in a formatting operation is that part of the system's record of files is erased. However, if the drive's file data is not erased (as is often the case) the evidence can be recovered by rebuilding the drive's file indexing. Rebuilding these directories or indexes can be difficult -- but not impossible.

The important point is that formatting a drive does not always destroy file data on the drive so it's often still there to be recovered by the computer forensics expert.

Wiped Disks

BEFORE WIPING

The woods are lovely, dark and deep. But I have promises to keep. And miles to go before I sleep.

Wiping effectively removes a file's data from the drive so that it can no longer be recovered. Software designed for wiping typically allows wiping an entire disk or logical parts of it (i.e. a folder and sub-folders or all unused space). Wiping overwrites every byte in the specified data areas,

replacing it with a particular character. It is easy to see why someone wishing to destroy evidence on a computer would want to use wiping software. Most operating systems in use today do not include software for wiping drives. That software is available, though, through private vendors and it's

AFTER WIPING

**XXXXXXXXXX
XXXXXXXXXXX
XXXXXXXXXXX
XXXXXXXX
XXXXXXXXXXX
XXXXXXXXXX
XXXXX**

reasonably inexpensive. Computer forensics experts regularly use wiping software to prepare the target hard drives onto which they copy suspect hard drives that have been selected for investigation.

Even wiping a drive does not always prevent the data on that drive from being read

WIPING: THE GOOD NEWS

- **Many don't know about it**
- **Some neglect to do it**
- **Intentional destruction may be evidence of guilt?**

by the FBI and others. The federal government has specialized precision machines that are able to read data from a drive even after it has been overwritten by other data five or more times. Federal security protocols specify that in the national interest, some drives containing sensitive information must be wiped up to seven times before the drives can be released for re-use.

Fortunately for law enforcement and others interested in recovering evidence from disk drives, only the most sophisticated (and paranoid) of computer users go to that extent in wiping evidence from their drives.

Defragmented Disks

In order that space on disk drives is used in the most efficient way, the drive's data areas are segmented into relatively small chunks. Only the smallest of files can be wholly contained in a single segment; most files span multiple segments. The most efficiently accessed files are those whose segments are contiguous and located close to the front of the drive. While the system attempts to store every file in contiguous segments, that is usually not possible. The segments comprising most files are not only not contiguous but are usually stored in segments scattered across a drive. Access to a file whose data is widely dispersed on a drive will be slower.

As new files are created on a drive, or existing files are accessed or modified, those files become fragmented. That is, they tend over time to be stored in smaller and smaller chunks that are scattered on the disk. The fragmentation of files slows down the system's file access, consequently slowing the system's operation. It is thus recommended that drives be occasionally defragmented.

Defragmentation[6] is the process that reconstitutes files so they are stored contiguously on the drive. The process attempts to place the segments of every file in a

---

[6] *Defragmenting a disk is often referred to as defragging.*

way that the file can be quickly accessed. Of course, it's not possible to place every segment optimally so a statistical technique computes a compromise location.

People who are trying to destroy computer evidence sometimes will defragment the drive thinking that data in files that have already been deleted will be overwritten. It's true that defragmentation is quite destructive of evidence – though not perfectly so. It is not unusual for fragments of previously deleted files to remain even after defragmentation because that process does not always completely overwrite unallocated space or slack space. It's not at all unusual for entire deleted files to be recovered.

> **THE GOOD NEWS ABOUT DEFRAGGING**
>
> - **Often not all unused segments are overwritten**
> - **Destroyed evidence is often found elsewhere**
> - **Intentional destruction looks bad for the culprit.**

Booby-Trapped Computers

To protect data they think might later become evidence, culprits sometimes booby-trap their computer. A booby-trap is usually a hostile piece of computer code that wipes out files or does damage to evidence. The hostile code may destroy critical data with great precision. Or the booby-trap could be an actual bomb that would physically damage the computer and its disks. There's no case on record of this being done but it is certainly possible.

The list of damage a booby-trap can do is long. A single file or an entire set of files can be erased or corrupted. The disks can be formatted, defragmented, or wiped. A booby-trap could release a virus, send threatening or harassing email, or even simply display a big message that says BANG!!!!![7]

Booby-traps can be triggered by any of many of the computer's system events or by some action or procedure executed by the culprit. The booby-trap triggering procedure could be as simple as a single key press or it could be a series of key presses known only to the culprit. Or, it could be triggered when an intruder (read this as *investigator*) fails to perform som e particular procedure -- such as turning the computer on or off without pressing a certain sequence of keys. It could be easy to blunder into

Figure 8-1   Four Windows Icons

triggering a booby-trap. For example, by simply clicking on a familiar desktop icon or by opening a familiar file. A trained computer forensics expert will always expect the worst and knows how to avoid such disasters.

---

[7] *I have heard of this actually happening.*

It isn't always computer forensics people who are the targets of booby-traps. The booby-trap could be created out of malice for some perceived slight and set to trigger when the system clock reaches a certain date/time. Consider the four icons in the upper-left corner of a Windows desktop screen -- as shown in Figure 8-1.

These icons seem harmless; two of them would look really enticing to an investigator. But be careful: the ones labeled *My Private Files* and *Client Database* are not what they seem. You can understand why a computer forensics investigator looking for evidence, say, of someone selling child pornography, would notice these two icons.

BOOBY-TRAP CAN BE TRIGGERED BY

- **Powering up**
- **Clicking on icon**
- **Clicking on program**
- **Opening a file**
- **Powering down**
- **Clock reaches a date**
- **Clock reaches a time**
- **Any key on keyboard**
- **Any computer event**

The investigator must beware. Because it is an easy task for any one knowledgeable about Windows systems to set things up so that a double click on any icon could trigger a booby-trap. In this case, the *My Private Files* icon is connected to a program that will defragment the hard drive. Clicking on the icon labeled *Client Database* would execute a small program designed to erase all files on all disks.

Just as someone trained in bomb-disposal, the computer forensics expert is always wary and not only avoids such booby-traps but easily uncovers them. On finding a booby-trap, the computer forensics investigator is only going to be more determined in

BOOBY-TRAP CAN BE SET TO

- Do physical damage
- Erase files
- Corrupt files
- Erase folders
- Format hard drives
- Defragment hard drives
- Release viruses
- Execute system commands
- Execute malicious codes
- And many others

his investigation. In the long run, the criminal who booby-traps his or her computer will only have provided more evidence of guilt.

Chapter

9

Computer Forensics Cases IV

Booby-Trapped Network

At 8:30 am on the m orning of July 31, 1996 an employee of a medium-sized manufacturing firm in New Jersey logged onto the company's network. Instead of gaining access to the network's programs and files as he expected, he saw a network message asking him to "be patient, the OS is being

Intel Pentium 4 Microchip

fixed." But instead of repairing the operating system as the message said, a booby-trap had been triggered and was completely wiping out not only critical computer programs but also the backups that had been consolidated on that computer.

The booby-trap was a logic bomb in the company's network server. It erased every copy of the company's one thousand tooling programs, programs that were necessary to the company's manufacturing processes. There were supposed to be other program backups on magnetic tape but it was soon discovered that the backup tapes were missing. Management called in the FBI.

```
        Please be patient.
    The OS is being fixed
```

The company was no longer able to manufacture any of the twenty-five thousand parts that had previously been available through their catalog. As a result, eighty employees were let go and ten million dollars in revenue lost. The incident brought the company almost to bankruptcy.

A computer forensics examination was immediately begun. Early results found that several weeks before the booby-trap was triggered, The company's Network Administrator had surgically removed the critical tooling programs from the company's database and moved them to the Network Server, a computer at company headquarters and the target of the booby-trap. The culprit had tried to remove or hide evidence of his crime. Never-the-less, fragments of the computer bomb program were found on the network computer. Experts were able to put these fragments together and reconstruct exactly how the bomb worked.

> ### DAMAGE FROM LOGIC BOMB
>
> - **Critical programs gone**
> - **Backup tapes missing**
> - **Production stopped**
> - **80 employees let go**
> - **$10 million lost**
> - **Company near bankruptcy**

Due to these facts and findings, computer forensics experts concluded that the culprit had to have been an expert on Novell Networks and they suspected the Network Administrator. He had previously checked out the network's only backup tapes and had not returned them.

The Network Administrator had been employed by there for eleven years prior to this disaster and had been Supervisor for six years. He had been well respected and for a time had thought of himself as their premier employee. But as a result of company mergers with several other firms he had been losing prestige. As a result he had become uncooperative and difficult to get along with. Management had ultimately demoted him from his supervisory position.

Suspecting he was about to be fired, the former Network Administrator consolidated all copies of critical computer programs on the network's file server. Then he requested and was given the only backup tapes. He took those tapes to his garage where they remained. When he was told a few weeks later that he was fired, he planted the booby-trap bomb in the central file server of the company's computer network, went home and waited. Three weeks later, the booby-trap was triggered when, on the target date, an unsuspecting employee logged onto the network.

A search of the former Network Administrator's garage revealed a dozen hard drives, hundreds of floppies, some computer hardware, and the two missing backup tapes. Computer forensics experts found the backup tapes had both been completely erased a few weeks after he was fired.

On one of the hard drives they found three versions of the destructive booby-trap program. They also found evidence that he had prepared the system message telling the employee who had inadvertently triggered the bomb that the "OS was being fixed."

The former employee was convicted of computer sabotage. He was sentenced to three years in prison and ordered to pay two million dollars in restitution.

EVIDENCE AGAINST THE CULPRIT

- **Moved critical programs**
- **The backup tapes:**
  - **Were in his garage**
  - **Had checked them out**
  - **Had not returned them**
  - **He had wiped them**
- **On his hard drive:**
  - **Versions of the bomb**
  - **Copy of warning note**

When it was learned that he would be able to pay back only one hundred dollars a month, the company observed (with feigned relief) that he would have the debt completely paid off by the year 3672.

A Mafia Key-Logger

Some mafia figures in the late nineties maintained records of their bookmaking and loan sharking activities by computer. These records they protected from law enforcement agencies and other snoopers by encrypting their most critical files. Aware of some of the illegal activities of these people, the FBI obtained search warrants giving them authority to search the contents of the gang's computer. There, they located a file that was protected by a popular encryption algorithm of the time called *PGP* ("Pretty Good Protection"'. Federal law enforcement agents thought that any file that was encrypted by these people would be of great importance to their prosecution.

After hours and hours of grinding, even the FBI's most powerful computers had not been able to crack the encryption of this file. FBI agents had to approach the discovery of the encryption key for this file in a different way – a more aggressive approach was required. So, agents applied to a U.S magistrate for a second warrant. This one authorized the FBI to install a key-logger on the mafia computer. A key-logger is computer software that, when installed on a computer, makes a log of every single keystroke that is struck on the computer's keyboard. The keystroke log can then be retrieved from the computer directly by means of physical access to the computer or via the Internet if the computer has an Internet connection. Once retrieved, the log can be studied to find out what inputs had been made to the computer through the keyboard during the period of the key-logger's residence on the computer.

Armed with the new warrant, FBI agents broke into the mob's offices and covertly installed the key-logger on the computer. The key-logger was in place only fourteen days before the file was opened again and the key-logger successfully recorded the required PGP passphrase (encryption key).

At first the FBI was stymied when the passphrase failed to open the suspect file. Further searching of the hard drive revealed a newer version of the file that had been encrypted with the passphrase. When this file was decrypted, the FBI had the evidence they needed. The leader of the gang was prosecuted and sentenced to prison.

Turns out, the encryption key was the Federal prison identification number of a former leader of the gang who was already serving a federal prison sentence.

This encryption key might have been guessed if guessing had been the only way the FBI had had of obtaining the key.

Cops vs. Kopp, Hidden Email Exchange

On October 23, 1998 Doctor Barnett Slepian was shot at his home with a Russian-made carbine. Dr. Slepian had been working at an abortion clinic and the FBI thought they knew who had shot him. James Kopp was a known anti-abortion activist and the FBI was pretty sure that was who had killed Dr. Slepian. In June 1999 the FBI placed Kopp's name on the nation's Ten Most Wanted list[8].

---

[8] *Interestingly, Osama Bin Laden's name was added at the same time.*

Kopp was able to leave the United States after the killing and was communicating with two suspected accomplices. The United States was on his trail though and that trail wound through several countries in South America and Europe. Throughout the chase the FBI was monitoring a web-based email account used by Kopp and the accomplices – but no actual emails were being transmitted.

Apparently Kopp and the accomplices suspected that emails sent over the Internet would be intercepted by the authorities. Kopp found a way to use the email account without actually sending any messages. Kopp would write and email to his friends but instead of pressing the SEND button, he would save the message in the draft folder. The accomplices could log onto the same email account and call up and read whatever was in the draft folder. They would in turn write and save their messages to Kopp in the draft folder. Kopp could then simply look in that folder to read their messages. In this way Kopp and his friends communicated by email without ever transmitting a message.

Of course, the FBI soon caught onto this technique and was able to subpoena from the Internet Service Provider not only the messages in the draft folder but also the IP addresses of the computers used to create the messages.

They asked law enforcement agents in France put surveillance on a certain cyber-café. Kopp was soon arrested by French police when he arrived at the café to pick up a package containing $300. After that it did not take the FBI long to locate and arrest Kopp's accomplices.

Kopp is now serving a life sentence.

Web-Surfing CEO

The Board of Directors of a mid-sized merchandising company hired an experienced CEO for the company when the previous man retired. The new CEO had a good record for producing company growth and appeared to be a good fit for the position; he was extensively vetted by the board before an offer in the high six figures was extended to him. The new CEO was in his mid-forties, had a vivacious wife and two teenage children. He accepted the offer and started work.

After the new CEO had been a on the job a year and a half the board became unhappy that the man was absent from the office so many day a week. Also, sales were falling with no apparent economic reason. After numerous discussions with the CEO, and after several months with no change in his behavior, the CEO was terminated by the Board. The CEO soon sued the company for wrongful termination.

Hoping to bolster their case against the CEO by finding evidence of wrongdoing, the Board instituted an investigation. The investigation included a detailed examination of the company's books and of the CEO's company computers; the Board engaged both their accounting firm and a computer forensics expert to conduct these activities.

The accounting firm submitted a preliminary report that an amount of money appeared to be unaccounted for; they recommended a full audit. The Board asked the computer forensics expert to search the computers for any evidence of unlawful or inappropriate expenditures executed by or authorized by the now former CEO.

Neither the audit nor the computer forensics expert turned up evidence of embezzlement or even of missing funds. The computer searches, though, did reveal that the CEO had spent hours and hours of company time surfing the Internet. Thousands of both heterosexual and homosexual pornographic images that had been downloaded from the Internet were found on the CEO's office computer.

Operational data on a computer frequently includes a cache of data showing Internet browsing history: a log which contains information on who was logged onto the computer at the time, addresses of Internet sites the user had visited, the date and time of each visit, and more. When a user logs onto a website, often that site will store on the visitor's computer a small record called a "cookie" that may also contain the date and time of the visit, the address of the site, information concerning the actions taken by the user during the visit -- and other information depending on the site visited.

This former CEO's computer did include much of the above described Operational data. So, in addition to the pornographic pictures on his computer, there was enough data relating to his web surfing proclivities to compile a very thorough history of his Internet surfing -- a surfing history complete with dates, times and web addresses. This history showed that he had spent many hours in his office during his work days over the past year searching for, viewing and downloading pornography.

When the discovery of all this material on his computer was revealed to him, the former CEO withdrew his lawsuit, apparently unwilling to risk the chance that his family would learn about how he had spent his time at work.

The Rigged Bidding Game

This case concerns the bidding process that two companies engaged in for a construction project. An executive from one of the construction companies (a man we'll call John) sent an email like the one of Figure 9-1 to another executive (who we'll call George) in a competitor's company.

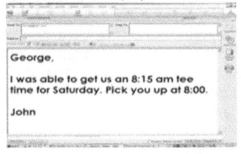

George,

I was able to get us an 8:15 am tee time for Saturday. Pick you up at 8:00.

John

Figure 9-1 Email as Normally Read

Changing the color of a message's font is a convenient trick for hiding information. For example, Figure 9-1 shows an email message that looks normal and straightforward and not at all suspicious. The actual wording that was sent in this message has been changed for purposes of illustration. John's management was suspicious because they had been losing an inordinate number of contracts to George's company by just a little margin. They knew the two men were friends so they had a computer forensics expert copy John's hard drive in the wee hours of the morning when John wasn't around. The expert discovered there was a hidden message in the email.

While the text of the message portion shown in Figure 9-1 was visible, the hidden part of message was not visible using normal viewing software because the writer of this message set the font color of the hidden part the same as the background color. That trick effectively made the final line invisible to email viewing software.

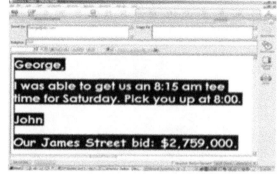

Figure 9-2   The Hidden Text Revealed

As can be seen in Figure 9-2, the expert read the hidden line by highlighting the entire page on which the message was displayed. On most email viewing software (but not all) the hidden line will stand out when highlighted.

For both John and George, the jig was up and both started interviewing for new jobs. The great hope is that they both went to work for the same company – no need then for sending secret emails to each other.

Chapter

10

Computer Forensics Examination

Principles

In computer forensics, a set of rigorous and disciplined procedures and techniques are employed to thoroughly examine a computer or other digital device using hardware and software designed specifically for such examinations. In spite of the disciplined nature of the  science, computer forensics requires flexibility and innovation by the investigator when handling unusual situations – something all too common in the computer sciences.

The use of special software is required in computer forensics examinations because the evidence sought often resides in places that cannot be accessed using standard computer programs available to the general public. The use of hardware tailored explicitly to computer forensics facilitates the attachment of a variety of digital devices to computer forensics investigative computers, provides portable acquisition equipment, and helps to preserve evidence in its original state.

The need for specific procedures arises partly because privacy and other laws govern what information may and what may not be legally obtained. Furthermore, in a computer forensics examination the evidence extracted may be required in a court of law or in some other official proceeding. The investigation must be conducted in a way that makes any potential contamination impossible. Even if not contaminated, evidence that is not obtained strictly according to accepted computer forensic procedures (including those that apply to chain of custody) can be attacked by the other side and may even be deemed inadmissible.

As you can see, there is more to computer forensics than just finding digital evidence. The sought information must be located and extracted without changing or corrupting any of the information in the computer. It must be done without introducing a virus to the target system. Once extracted, the evidence must be authenticated. The expert must be able to show that evidence obtained was not itself modified in the process of its extraction.

The results of an examination must be presented completely and without prejudice; both inculpatory and exculpatory evidence must be presented. Technical evidence, which is often quite complex, must not be misrepresented and must be presented in a way that is easily understood.

Privacy Rights

It is not possible to just search someone's computer without the concern that you may be violating their privacy rights. Law enforcement will likely need a search warrant to obtain evidence from a personally owned computer unless it has been seized at a crime scene under pertinent authority. It is possible that a user would consent to a search but that's unlikely if that user really had evidence of a crime on his or her computer.

In the private sector, things can be simpler – except in the case of email, which will be discussed presently. A company that owns the computers used by their employees can put in place company-wide policies that are signed by every employee. They can also place banners on their employee's computer screens reiterating the policy. Such practices can remove the employees' expectation of privacy and, if handled properly, the company is usually within their rights to authorize a search of any of their computers at any time – even if the search must be done surreptitiously.

With email, the situation is a little different. An employee's expectation of privacy is extended by law to the point that the person to whom the email is addressed downloads the email to their machine. If the email has not been downloaded from the company's network server or from the Internet Service Provider, a court order would be required for others to gain access. If an examiner has a right to search a computer, he may access any email that has already been downloaded by the user to whom it's addressed.

Many details have been skimmed over in this section --
and any particular case may be complicated by any of a
number of factors. If there is any uncertainty as to the
privacy rights of individuals, it's important to consult an
attorney before attempting access.

Conduct of the Examination

If you decide to engage a computer forensics expert,
remember that coaxing the last tiny bit of forensic
information from a computer requires intensive training and
years of living with the processes that are required for the
creation, processing and retrieval of computer information. It
also requires an intricate understanding of the electronic
equipment on which and by which information is stored.

When you have found the computer forensics expert
you'd like to use, a letter of engagement is first signed by the
parties. Most computer forensic investigations are begun by
making an exact bit-by-bit copy of all electronic media
whether it is one or more hard disks, floppy disks, or other.
Exact duplicates of the original media will be made so that
evidence recovery can be performed on copies and not on
the originals. An accepted forensic procedure will be used to
make an exact copy of the original media onto forensically
sterile media. Thus, you may have confidence that any
evidence recovered actually exists on the original media,
that everything was done to minimize the risk of its
alteration, and that no evidence was missed. Rigorous
chain-of-custody procedures are maintained.

As the work proceeds, newly uncovered leads and intermediate findings will be reported to you as they occur. You may decide that certain of the originally agreed tasks should be eliminated or modified or that additional ones should be undertaken. If that happens, revised estimates of time and cost will be proffered for authorization and an addendum to the letter of engagement prepared. The process of review and changes may be repeated as often as required. It's important that both parties are always clearly in agreement as to the scope of the inquiries and that you are assured that each of your concerns have been addressed.

Special forensic hardware, software and procedures will be used to find evidence that may have been deleted, hidden, encrypted or obscured. It may be necessary to break passwords, scan logs of internet sites visited or even search the internet for additional information. Throughout the investigation, the computer forensics expert will try to infer the computer user's intentions. If there is both inculpatory and exculpatory evidence on the computer, the examiner is duty-bound to reveal both.

Final Report of Examination

When the examination is complete, procedures used and examination results will be documented and reported. Recovered evidence will be provided both in hardcopy and on CD or other electronic media as required. The report may include tables, graphics, charts or other materials to present all findings clearly and comprehensively. When appropriate, expert interpretation of the evidence will be provided and the report will include everything needed by the client to make an informed decision as to how to proceed with the case.

Other information deemed pertinent to the examination will be reported – for example: who uses the computer, addresses of internet sites recently visited, when the computer was last turned on or off, who is the author of certain documents, whether the disk was formatted or defragmented and when, and which files had been deleted. Also included will be the date/time of creation, modification, access and deletion of files when those are available.

Copies of deleted files and file fragments that have been recovered will also be provided as will the passwords and unprotected versions of password-protected files. To the extent practical, the contents of databases and other documents will be presented in table form and may also be imported to spreadsheets. Examination results can also be presented orally.

Chapter

11

The Case of the Black Baron

> Your hard disk is being corrupted courtesy of PATHOGEN! Programmed in the U.K. (Yes, NOT Bulgaria!) [C] the Black Baron 1993-94. Featuring SMEG v0.1: Simulated Metamorphic Encryption Generator! 'Smoke me a kipper, I'll be back for breakfast.....' Unfortunately some of your data won't!!!!!"

The Crimes

In the early nineties, computers throughout the Internet began displaying the message noted above in the box under the title to this chapter.

Computers and networks on the Internet had mysteriously begun contracting two odd viruses that wiped out files on a victim's computer. One of the viruses, as noted in the box above, identified itself as *Pathogen*. The other was called *Queeg*. The two viruses were known to Scotland

Yard's elite Computer Crime Unit at Holborn but were nevertheless doing much damage.

The viruses' startup messages were signed by someone calling himself "The Black Baron." The Black Baron, in a not-so-amusing irony, had hidden the viruses in a popular piece of AntiVirus software and was uploading it to hacked computer networks and Bulletin Boards from which it could be downloaded for free. He was also installing Pathogen and Queeg in a variety of programs and uploading these free, virus-infected, downloadable programs to various sites on the Internet.

VIRUSES HIDDEN ON INTERNET

- PATHOGEN - virus
- QUEEG - virus
- SMEG - virus production kit
- Hidden in anti-virus software
- Uploaded to bulletin boards
- Uploaded to networks

The viruses, when triggered, would wipe out files on a victim's computer – in some case, all files. More troubling to authorities though was the fact that he was also distributing a virus kit that enabled other virus writers to more easily hide their viruses through a series of encryption algorithms. He had named this do-it-yourself virus encryption kit "SMEG." Using SMEG, a virus writer would cause his virus to encrypt itself using a different encryption algorithm each time it replicated itself on someone's computer. This technique, known as "polymorphism," if it continued to be used and more widely propagated over a long period, promised to confound antivirus efforts. But, the Black Baron had overlooked something.

The Apprehension

Through carelessness on the part of the Black Baron, police at the Scotland Yard Computer Crimes Unit had been able to determine the phone number from which these attacks were being launched. That phone number led them to Christopher Pile, a young man in his early twenties residing with his parents in one of a tidy row of houses overlooking the sea in Devon, England. Through a little research regarding Pile, detectives learned, among other things, that he had an associate and that the names Pathogen, Queeg and Smeg were associated with a TV series of the period called "Red Dwarf."

When the Scotland Yard detectives and their computer forensics expert, half a dozen men and women in all, knocked on the door of Pile's home with a search warrant, the young man calmly showed them in; his mother offered the visitors a cup of tea. When the detectives informed Pile that they were there to investigate his possible violation of the country's Computer Misuse Act, Young Pile did not seem surprised but politely claimed he did not have a computer.

A thorough search of the house turned up nothing tying Pile to a computer or to the TV series Red Dwarf. There was no computer, no diskettes, no incriminating computer books; nothing – though the investigators were pretty sure a computer had recently been removed from a now empty table in Pile's bedroom. One group of detectives escorted Pile to the Charles Cross Police Station for further questioning while another group headed to the home of Pile's associate.

A search of the home of Pile's associate (who appeared to be a games programmer working from his bedroom) revealed several computers, one stashed in a sealed cardboard box with a keyboard, mouse, some relevant software documentation and about fifty floppies. All the computers along with the keyboard, mouse and floppies were seized by the law enforcement team and taken to the police station along with the associate.

The Forensic Examination

When he arrived at the police station Pile was relieved of his belt, shoelaces and shoes – just for safety's sake. Neither Pile nor the associate, having arrived at different times and placed in separate interview rooms, knew the other was there at the station and being interviewed. Pile was joined by his attorney in the interview room.

CONCEALED EVIDENCE FOUND

- Desktop computer
- Tens of floppies
- Software documentation
- Found in friend's closet
- Concealed in sealed box

Upon returning to the police station, the computer forensics expert got to work immediately on the computer's hard drives and on the floppies. Alone in the Fraud Squad Office near the interview rooms, he worked quickly so as to be able to assist the detectives questioning the two suspects. They wanted evidence to help direct their questioning so there wasn't time at first to delve too deeply into the contents of the computers or diskettes.

Just an overview would be a good start. So he searched based only on the scant information they already had: the suspect's names, the virus' and encryption programs' names and known footprints, and some keywords from the accompanying documentation.

On the first preliminary examination of the computers, the computer forensics expert found nothing incriminating until he got to the last computer, the one they had found in the cardboard box. That one had been recently defragmented and the deleted files wiped. He knew there were valid reasons for a computer user to defragment his computer – and valid reasons, too, to wipe deleted files. Nevertheless, under the present circumstances, this was a red flag and he would make it known to the detectives.

He also located and innocent-looking job application letter from Chris Pile to British Rail. This letter, which included a recent date, did not appear to relate directly to the virus infections but it did tie Pile to the cardboard box computer – and, by association, to the diskettes. The computer forensics expert printed a copy of the letter and took it, along with a note detailing the defragging and the wiping, to the detectives interviewing Pile.

Pile's Initial Statement

Pile had already told the interview team that he had not owned a computer and knew nothing of the viruses. He had claimed that he had worked from home for a few months as a games programmer, had recently given up the job and returned the computer to his former employer. As pile was about to sign a copy of the statement he had given, a detective produced the job application letter. Pile reacted by asking to be alone with his attorney. The detectives all left the room.

Pile's New Statement

When they returned after a few minutes, Pile's attorney told the detectives that Pile would like to start over with a new statement. The original statement was discarded and they started again. This time Pile stated that he had, in fact, owned the computer, that he had quarreled with his father over the computer and so had decided to sell it. He said that he wished to avoid further conflict with his father over the computer so he told his father that the computer had already been sold. Pile said he had asked his friend only to hide the computer until it could be sold. He claimed had had not

known he was breaking the law by his access to the Internet Bulletin Board Systems and networks. He further claimed he had had no knowledge of (or responsibility for) the viruses.

While Pile's interrogation continued, the computer forensics investigator restarted his examination with renewed vigor, this time delving even deeper into the contents of the computer. He searched in particular for compressed, encrypted and password protected files and folders – whose contents would not have been noticed on his earlier searches. Other than the presence on the hard drive of two computer programs (the first named *Encrypt* and the second named *Decrypt*) nothing of interest to the case was found. The two programs (*Encrypt* and *Decrypt*) did raise some serious interest though and when he tested them he was able to conclude that they did in fact encrypt and decrypt files.

With the hard drive part of his examination finished, the computer forensics expert turned his attention to the floppies that had been found in the cardboard box along with a computer mouse. One of the floppies had a label that indicated that it contained a mouse driver (a system program –

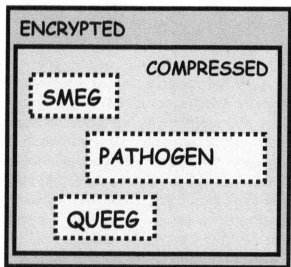

one that a computer's operating system would use in the control of the computer's mouse). Of the several files on that floppy just one seemed out of place, a file named *mouse.dat* and it had been encrypted. Suspicious? Oh yes! Why would anyone encrypt a mouse driver or any of its supporting files? It would have to be decrypted to find out exactly what it was. But its decryption would require the encryption key and only Pile had that.

Pile's *New* New Statement

Pile's associate had been sent home; detectives had convinced themselves that he had simply stored Pile's computer as a favor to his friend and was not a party to Pile's activities.

The information about the encrypted file *mouse.dat* was whispered to the lead interrogator who only nodded without changing his expression. Pile had completed the second version of his statement and was about to sign it when the interrogator casually asked why the hard drive had been defragged and the deleted files wiped.

Pile seemed stunned. After another private consultation with his attorney Pile asked to rewrite his statement a second time and the process was begun again -- again. At this time Pile stated that he had deleted all his personal files on the computer before giving it to his friend for safekeeping in preparation for selling. He had wanted his own files off the computer when someone else bought it. As so often happens with those trying to conceal evidence, the job of concealment was less than perfect and Pile had overlooked the file with the job application letter.

As the questioning proceeded, detectives queried Pile on the technical aspects of defragging, wiping and other issues. Though reluctant to talk about such things, Pile did answer the questions, thus revealing a yet deeper level of understanding of the workings of computers than he had previously admitted.

Pile's *Final* New Statement

When the law enforcement agents prepared to release Pile on his own recognizance, Pile noticeably relaxed. Only then did the lead interrogator ask Pile for the encryption key for the file *mouse.dat.*

This caused Pile some concern but eventually he provided the encryption key to the file *mouse.dat.* The key he gave was *enginedriver.* Again he asked to prepare still another new statement.

Meanwhile, the computer forensics expert applied the key *enginedriver* to the decryption of *mouse.dat* and found that the file, once decrypted, contained a ZIP compression file. Decompression was trivial and quick. Once completed, it revealed that several files had been compressed. The first of these was named *smeg.asm.* When this file was opened and the first line of the code displayed, the screen showed the following.

The Simulated Metamorphic Encryption Generator

Copyright "The Black Baron"

The other files compressed with *smeg.asm* were all related to smeg.asm and to the virus programs, *Pathogen* and *Queeg.* Police now had the proof they would need to convict the Black Baron.

Pile's Confession

Confronted with this overwhelming evidence The Black Baron confessed to his crimes; he admitted creating the viruses and distributing them on various bulletin board systems. He claimed he had no other reason for these crimes other than that had wanted to "make his mark."

The Black Baron was released from prison after serving eighteen months working in the prison laundry. He had paid for his crimes.

Chapter

12

The Computer Forensics Expert

The Trained and Certified Expert

There is more to a computer forensics investigation than just collecting digital evidence. A trained computer forensics examiner will protect the integrity of the original evidence. Nothing will be done that changes or compromises the evidence in any way. The examiner will use accepted forensic

procedures and forensically   Forensic Exam Computer
sterile media during the
examination. Any evidence copied will be copied to media that is free of any data, virus or defect that might show up during the examination and be mistaken for part of the original evidence. The examiner will be able to testify

confidently that any evidence he found during the examination must have been present on the original media.

A trained computer forensics examiner will maintain the chain of custody at all times for all evidence whether it be original evidence or evidence derived during the examination. Any software, hardware or procedure used during the examination will have been tested ahead of time by the examiner. Every step of the examination will be documented in the examiner's notes in a manner that enables him or her to later recall exactly what was done.

Danger: The Uncertified Expert

It is imperative that a computer forensics examination be executed in a forensically sound manner using forensically sterile media and correct forensic procedures. Otherwise, the evidence could be contaminated, subject to attack, or ruled inadmissible.

In-house IT professionals, data-recovery professionals and private investigators may lack the training, hardware and software required to conduct forensically sound investigations of computers. An investigation by in-house IT professionals could result in allegations of fabrication of evidence or other impropriety. Could an untrained and uncertified professional qualify in court as an expert in the field of computer forensics? Probably not. And if not, they would not be allowed to render opinions or conclusions.

If your computer forensics examination results in an employee termination or disciplinary action, civil litigation may follow. Better to err on the side of caution and be ready for any eventuality.

There are many information technologists who know about computers, disk drives, digital memory and the like. Many of them probably know how to recover deleted evidence and perhaps even some of the hidden evidence.

AN UNTRAINED EXAMINER MIGHT:

- **Destroy evidence**
- **Corrupt evidence**
- **Overlook evidence**
- **Not crack passwords**
- **Trigger booby trap**
- **Crash computer**
- **Introduce virus**
- **Spawn lawsuits**
- **Produce inadmissible evidence**

However, there are serious risks to using untrained people who are unschooled in forensic protocols. They could destroy, corrupt or overlook evidence; they could fail to crack passwords or encryption keys; they could trigger a booby-trap; introduce a virus; render evidence inadmissible. Destruction of important evidence will likely occur by turning a computer on or off if correct forensic procedures are not used. If any of the missteps related above occur, a lawsuit could be the result.

If there is any doubt about the future course of a computer forensics investigation, it's safest to call upon a trained and certified computer forensics expert.

Appendix

Glossary

Bit. A bit is the smallest unit of data in a computer or on a disk. It is formally known as a binary bit and can take on only one of two values, zero or one (hence the name binary).

Byte. A byte is a small amount of computer memory -- somewhat more than required to uniquely represent any one of the following: alphabetic letters (upper and lower case), the numbers zero to nine, any punctuation, and any of a hundred special characters. On most personal computers today, a byte is eight bits.

Cluster. A cluster is a grouping of sectors. A cluster may be as small as one sector (on a floppy disk, there is one sector per cluster). Although a file may consist of a very large number of clusters the smallest file on a FAT-based disk is one cluster.

Date/Time Stamp. When Windows creates a file, a directory (or sub-directory) entry is made to describe this file to the operating system. The entry is date/time-stamped (meaning that the date and time of certain file events are logged in the entry). File name is part of the entry as is file size, date/time of creation, date/time of modification and date/time of last access.

Decryption. A process whereby an encrypted computer file or other entity is rendered once again readable by replacing each character of the encrypted tract with the original character of the original readable version. The result of decryting a file is a plaintext version of the file.

Deleted File. A deleted file is a file that has been marked as no longer needed. When a file is deleted the File Allocation Table or MFT entry for that particular file is changed to mark the file space available for use by a new file. Nothing is done to the Data Area; data in the Data Area remains unchanged until overwritten by a new file or until wiped.

Directory (and Subdirectory). Directories and subdirectories are often called "Folders." A directory in a FAT-based system is an index with an entry for every non-deleted file. A file's entry in a directory, among other things, tells the system where to look for the file's location on the disk. There can be many directories on one disk. Directories are arranged in a hierarchical manner. The top-level directory on a disk is called the root directory. A subdirectory is any directory that is not the root directory -- so it occurs at some level below the root directory. Any directory (even a subdirectory) may itself contain subdirectories.

Encryption. A process whereby a computer file or other entity is rendered unreadable by substituting each character of the original entity with an apparently nonsense character.

Encryption Key. An encryption key is a word or sequence of words that are used to control the encryption of a computer file or other entity. The same encryption key used in the encryption algorithm is

required to decrypt the item so that it can again be
made readable.

FAT. FAT is the acronym for File Allocation Table.

File Allocation Table (FAT). A FAT is an artifact of
certain data storage systems in which the content of
files may be stored in a discontiguous manner, where
groups of data bytes may be distributed throughout the
sectors and clusters of a hard disk or floppy disk. The
FAT is constructed by the system to maintain
information about where each segment of bytes is
stored. Use of the FAT enables the system to perfectly
reassemble any file whenever it is needed. There is
always a backup copy of the FAT on the disk. The two
FAT copies are referred to as FAT 1 and FAT 2.

There are several versions of FATs: FAT12, FAT16
and FAT32 for instance. These variations in FAT
designations refer to the length of each entry in the
FAT and consequently to the maximum effective size
of a disk to which that particular FAT may refer.

File Compression. A process whereby files are able to
be stored in less space on a disk drive or other medium
– hence the terms "compressed." With some
algorithms, compression can be accomplished without
any loss of the original information in the file.

File Creation (and Storage). When a file is created
three things occur: 1) An entry is made into the File
Allocation Table (FAT) or to the MFT to indicate where
the actual data is stored in the Data Area. 2) A
directory entry is made to indicate file name, size, date

and time of creation, date and time of last modification, the last access date, and other information. 3) The file data is written to the Data Area.

File Fragment. If data from a deleted file resides in unallocated clusters in the data area of a disk drive and some of those clusters are subsequently overwritten by a new file, a fragment of the original file may remain in the in the original clusters that had not been overwritten. Such a file fragment can be recovered. Please note that the term "file fragment" also includes the case where the fragment is actually the complete file (all the file data is present.)

File Slack. When a file is written to a disk drive, it writes in sector sized chunks. But when space is allocated for a file, it is allocated in cluster sized chunks. This can result in some files occupying only some sectors of the final cluster at the end of the file. The sectors of the last cluster that are not overwritten may contain a fragment of the previous file that was allocated to the cluster. That portion of the cluster that is not overwritten by the new file is called file slack. Any residual data (data that was there before this new file was copied) in the file slack area will remain unchanged and is recoverable.

File System. File System is the name given to the software that handles computer operation concerning files (for instance, file creation, deletion etc.). The File System is a normal adjunct to the Operating System. Two common file systems associated with the Windows operating systems are one called FAT and another known as NTFS.

Gigabyte. Hard drive capacity is measured in gigabytes (nominally, billions of bytes). A gigabyte (GB) is somewhat more than a thousand-million bytes. A gigabyte is 1,073,741,824 bytes.

Key-Logger. A key-logger is software that can be placed on (or downloaded to) a computer. Obviously, for someone to place it directly on the computer they must have physical access to that computer. A key-logger's function is to make a log of every key that is struck on the computer's keyboard. That log can then be uploaded via the Internet to a computer somewhere. Alternatively, someone can copy the log onto removable media if they are able to gain physical access to the computer.

MFT. The MFT is the acronym for Master File Table. The MFT is a component of an NTFS system.

Master File Table. The object used in the NTFS file system to keep track of the locations and other administrative details concerning files placed on a disk drive.

Metadata. Metadata is stored within the file. It contains information about the file, its author and the environment in which the file exists.

NTFS. A common file system. NTFS stands for New Technology File System.

O.S. O.S. is the acronym for Operating System.

Operating System. The computer code that controls and coordinates the overall operations of the computer. For example, Windows 2000, Windows XP, Windows Vista and others are operating systems.

Password. A password is a word that is used to control access to a computer, a file or any other entity. A password serves the same function as a key does to a lock.

Passphrase. Another name for an encryption key – especially when the key consists of more than one word. An encryption key is a word or sequence of words that are used to control the encryption of a computer file or other entity. The same encryption key used in the encryption algorithm is required to decrypt the item to return it to plaintext so that it can again be made readable.

Plaintext. Plaintext is the name given to a message, file or other that is either not encrypted or that has been decrypted.

Real Time Clock. The Real Time Clock (RTC) is a computer chip located on the computer motherboard that keeps track of the current date and time. It is powered by an internal battery so that it continues to keep time when the computer's power is off.

Recycle Bin. Files are normally deposited in the Recycie Bin when you ask the system to delete them. For a deleted file to actually disappear, the Recycle Bin must be emptied. Only then are the files in the Recycle Bin deleted (and even then the data in the file may persist until another file's data overwrites it).

RTC. RTC is the acronym for the Real Time Clock.

Sector. A sector is a grouping of data bytes on a disk. For example, there are 512 bytes in a sector on a FAT-based floppy diskette. There may be more bytes on a hard drive formatted in any file system.

Slack. Files are written to a disk drive in segments of a specific size. If a file does not fill the whole final segment, then unfilled space remains at the end of the segment. That space is called file slack and it may contain fragments of previous files.

Steganography. The process whereby one file is stored within another. Steganography is normally done to hide the interior file from discovery.

Swap File. An operating system's swap files are its virtual memory. They enable the system to use its immediate memory more effectively and may contain evidence.

Temporary File. Many applications create temporary files that contain copies of user data. These files are used temporarily by an application and are not meant to be permanent files (though they sometimes inadvertently remain after the application is exited).

Unallocated Space (or Unused Space). The parts of a disk drive not allocated to a file or other system use.

ZIP. A particular format for compressing files. The word is sometimes used as a verb; as in "The file has been zipped."

Wiper Programs. Wiper programs are computer programs whose object is to overwrite files' data areas with nonsense data. Wiping renders the data formerly occupying the space very difficult (if not impossible) to recover. Wiper programs are used to overcome the fact that the process of deleting a file does not remove the contents of the file -- it does not remove a file's data. Wiper programs can also overwrite all of unallocated spaced so that nothing of its former contents can be recovered without using extraordinary means.

INDEX

C

M

N

O

P

Z